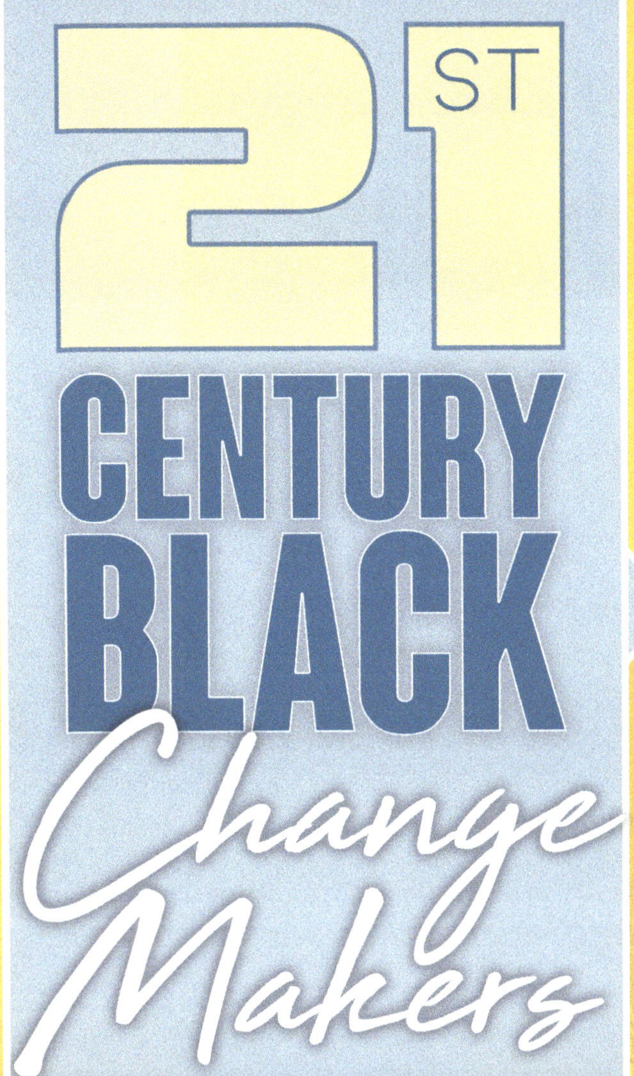

21ST CENTURY BLACK
Change Makers

By **Daniel J. Middleton**

Biography Coloring

UNIQUE COLORING

Layout and Design by Daniel J. Middleton

First published in the United States in July 2021 by Unique Coloring. Printed by Ingram Book Group, LLC.

ISBN: 978-1-935702-43-6 (Trade Paperback)

1 2 3 4 5 6 7 8 9 10   IBG   25 24 23 22 21

VISIT US ONLINE:
www.uniquecoloring.com

INTRODUCTION

Welcome to Biography Coloring, where you will learn of a few interesting and noteworthy black individuals who have effected change through their efforts while being able to color them! The twelve subjects presented herein will come in full-color versions for reference as well as grayscale illustrations ready for your color application. Unlike many grayscale coloring books on the market, which simply convert color images into grayscale, this book's coloring pages were designed specifically for coloring in mind. To that end, I have remained within strict tonal and shading parameters to allow for the best coloring experience.

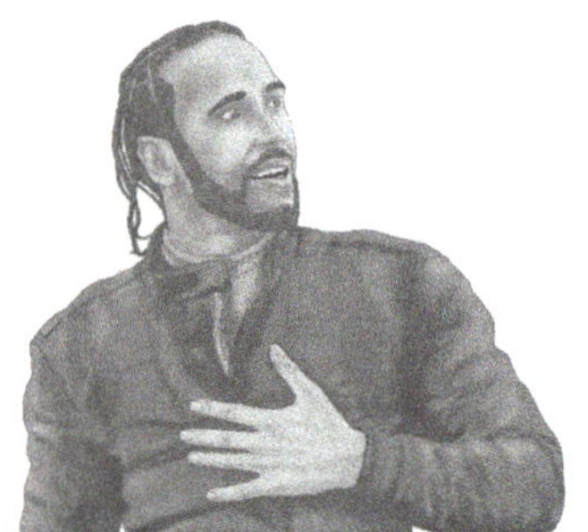

Image converted from color

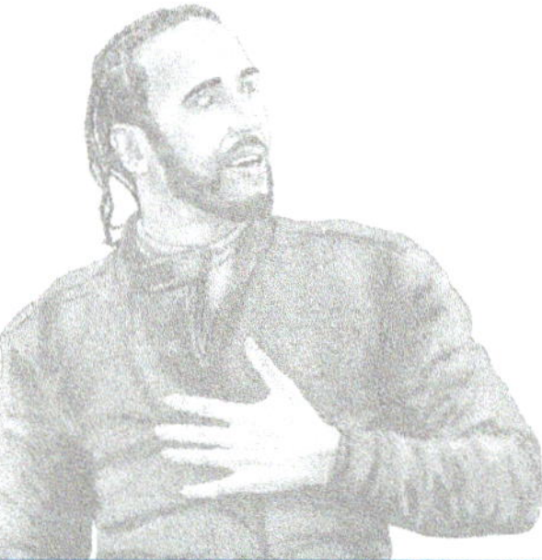

Image illustrated specifically to be colored

Color each illustration using light mediums, such as colored pencils or quality crayons. If you prefer to use watercolors, pastels, markers, and heavier mediums, either apply a backing to the coloring pages before laying down color, or feel free to cut out the coloring pages and copy them to your paper of choice. Send me your finished artwork by taking digital photographs or scanning them. Then email me with the subject line 21ST CENT.

CHANGEMAKERS IN COLOR, and attach and send the artwork to the address below so it can be featured on the website:

uniquecoloring@gmail.com

With all of the preliminaries out of the way, I bid you happy reading and coloring!

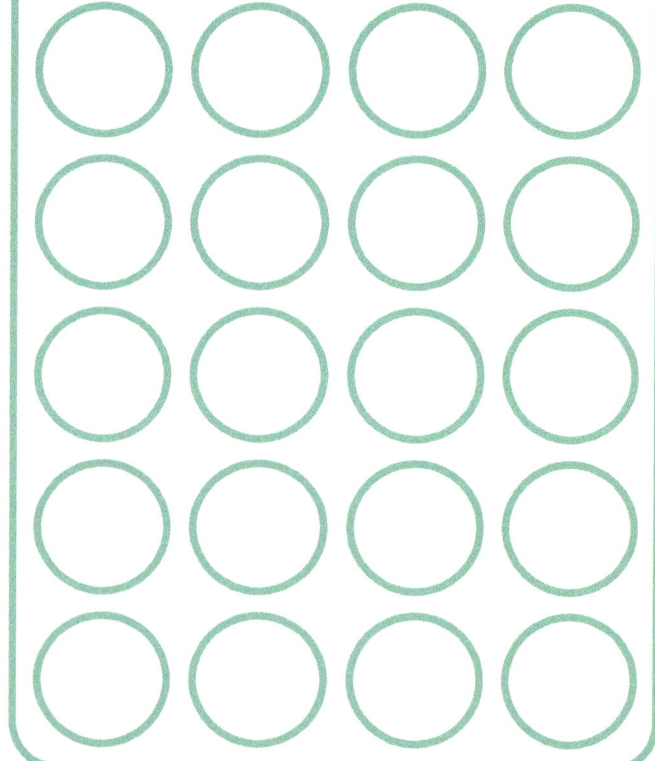

TEST YOUR COLORS

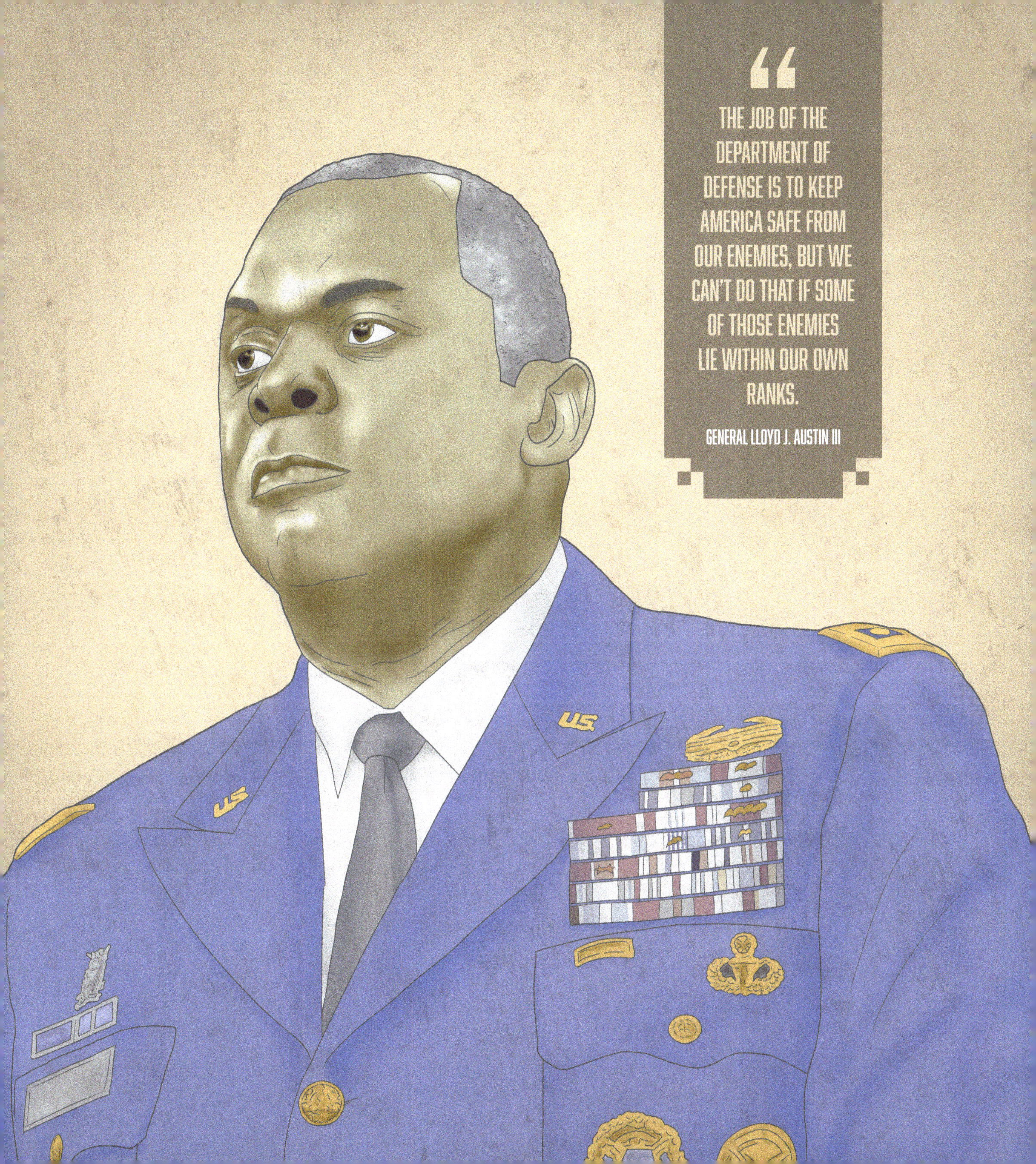

"
THE JOB OF THE DEPARTMENT OF DEFENSE IS TO KEEP AMERICA SAFE FROM OUR ENEMIES, BUT WE CAN'T DO THAT IF SOME OF THOSE ENEMIES LIE WITHIN OUR OWN RANKS.
GENERAL LLOYD J. AUSTIN III
US.
US.

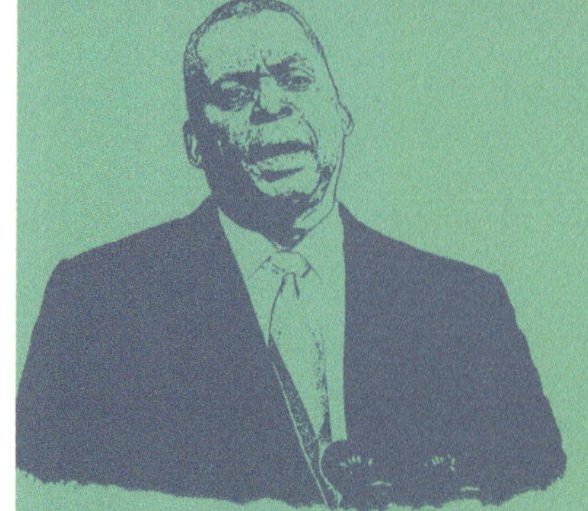

GEN. LLOYD AUSTIN

After serving a distinguished military career, Lloyd James Austin III, a retired four-star Army general, was sworn in as the 28th secretary of defense on January 22, 2021. Austin served a total of 41 years in the military following his graduation at West Point, the U.S. Military Academy in upstate New York. While his confirmation as the first black secretary of defense is indeed a high historic point for Austin, his career is full of several firsts.

He commanded troops in active combat at all four levels in the office of general, and at the height of his career, he commanded an entire theater of war, being the first black American in history to hold that distinction. That post, which is an important division of the Department of Defense known as U.S. Central Command, left Austin in charge of U.S. military strategy and joint operations in the Middle East and Central and South Asia, covering a total area of 4 million square miles. As the Combined Forces Commander, Austin oversaw military efforts in the fight against ISIL, the terrorist organization in Iraq and Syria. In 2012, Austin made history again by serving as the vice chief of staff of the Army, being the first black person to hold that rank—the second highest in the service.

Lloyd Austin was born in Mobile, Alabama in 1953, but his family later moved and raised him in Thomasville, Georgia. After being introduced to Catholicism by his mother, a devout observer of the faith, Austin continued in the religion. He graduated from West Point in 1975 with a Bachelor of Science degree and was commissioned in Infantry as a second lieutenant. His first assignment took him overseas to Germany, where he served with the 3rd Infantry Division. He later served with the 82nd Airborne Division at Fort Bragg, North Carolina as well as the 10th Mountain—Light Infantry—Division at Fort Drum, New York, completing the Infantry Officer Advanced Course and earning his master's degree from Auburn University in the interim. Another master's (this time in business administration) was earned from Webster University in 1989.

After 41 years of service, Lloyd Austin retired on April 5, 2016, with a ceremony held at Joint Base Myer–Henderson Hall in Arlington, Virginia. In retirement, he joined the boards of several companies, such as Raytheon Technologies, a military contractor; Nucor, a Charlotte, North Carolina-based producer of steel, and Tenet Healthcare. He also launched a consulting firm, Austin Strategy Group, LLC, in Great Falls, Virginia.

While he was shy of being retired for the 7 years required by law for prospective defense secretaries, both the House of Representatives and the Senate passed a waiver for the law in favor of Austin. He became the third secretary of defense in history to be granted such a waiver, following five-star general George Marshall in 1950 and Trump appointee James Mattis in 2017.

After being confirmed, Austin tweeted:

> "It's an honor and a privilege to serve as our country's 28th Secretary of Defense, and I'm especially proud to be the first African American to hold the position. Let's get to work."

Lloyd Austin is married to Charlene Denise Banner, who has been his wife since 1980. Ⓤ

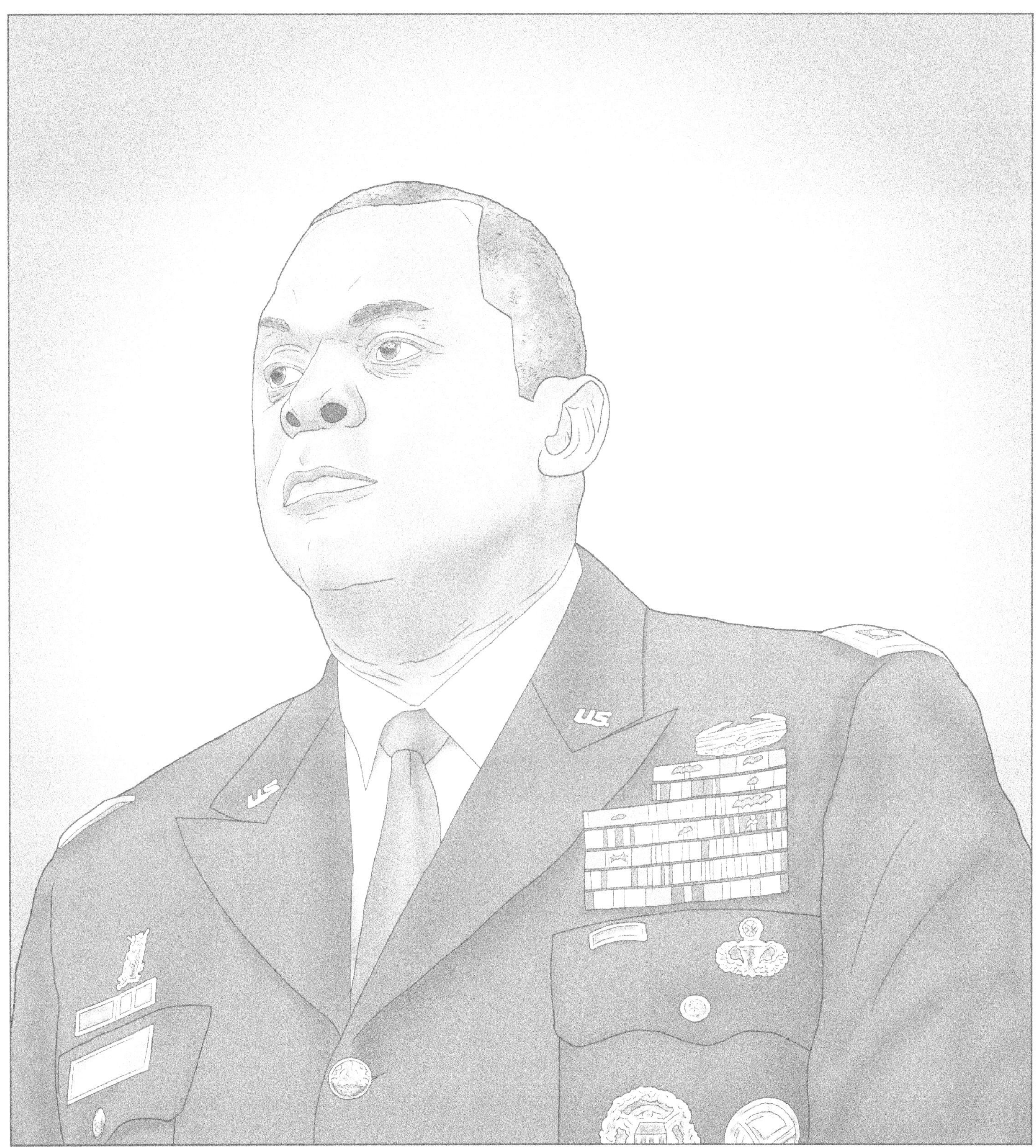

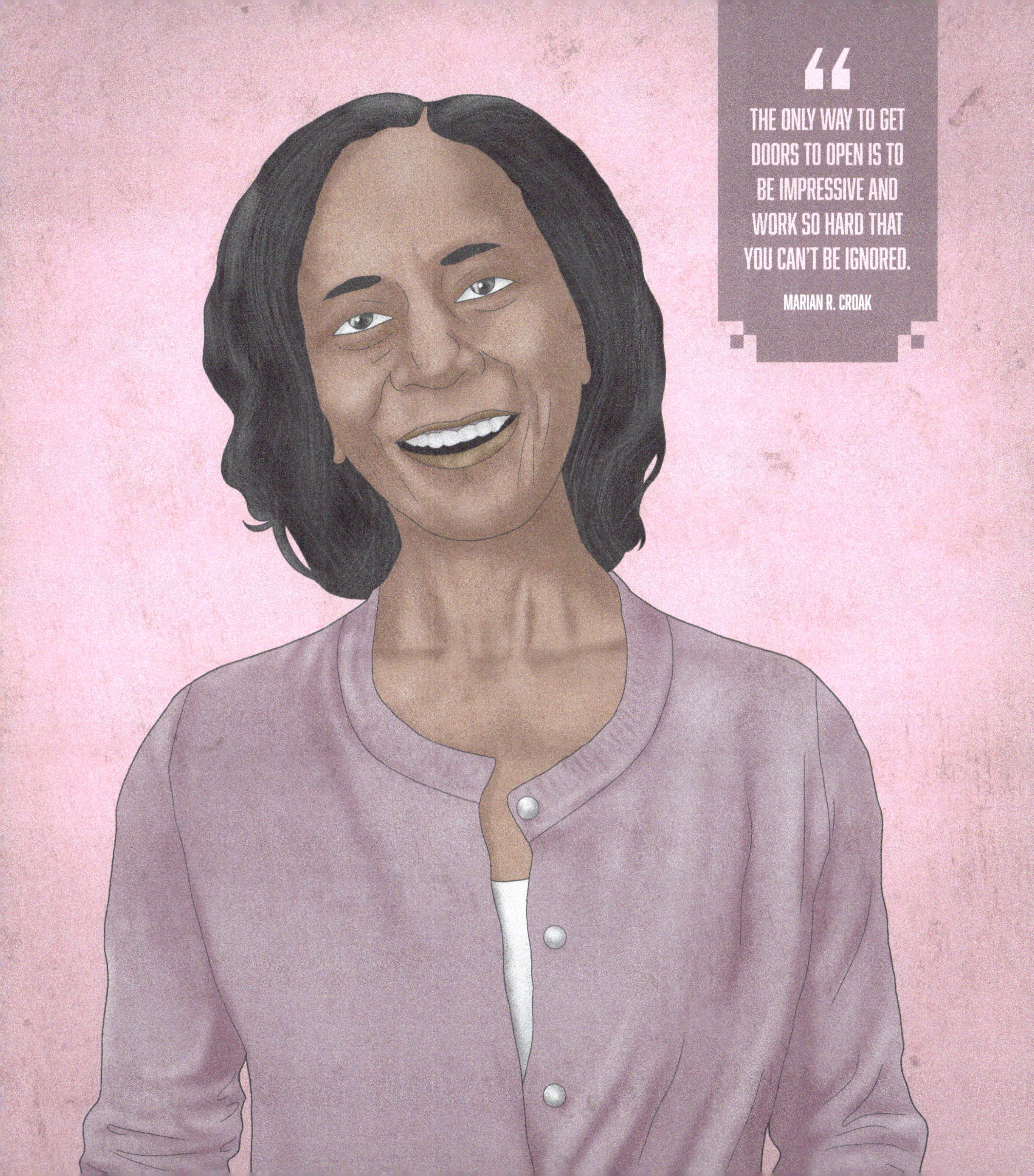
"
THE ONLY WAY TO GET
DOORS TO OPEN IS TO
BE IMPRESSIVE AND
WORK SO HARD THAT
YOU CAN'T BE IGNORED.
MARIAN R. CROAK

MARIAN R. CROAK

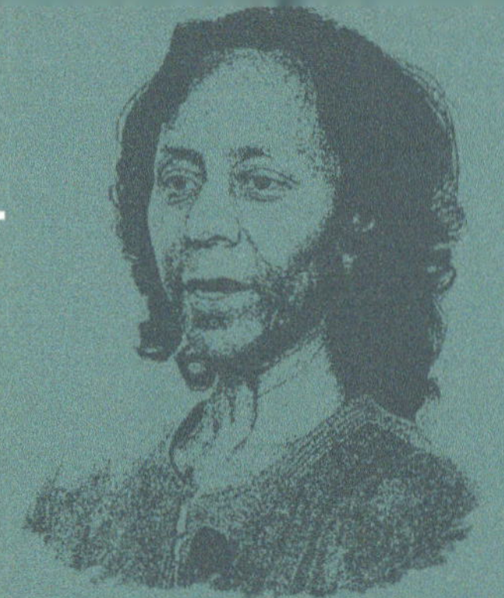

Marian R. Croak may not be a household name, but the technologies she helped develop have narrowed the world through a revolutionary communication method: VoIP (Voice over Internet Protocol). Marian rose to become the vice president of engineering at Google, making her one of the highest-ranking people among its 200,000+ workforce (including contract workers). She also holds over 200 patents, nearly half of which relate to VoIP. The technology allows people to make calls over the internet through a computer, and many large corporations have adopted the service.

Marian R. Croak was born in Pennsylvania in 1955, but she carefully guards her private life, particularly her early years. During a summit, she revealed she grew up in New York. As a young girl, when things broke in the house, her father usually called repair people, who were always men. Marian admits to being fascinated by these experts as she followed them around the house while they tinkered with things. This experience sparked her desire to be a "fixer."

"That has stayed with me all my life,"
Marian recalled. "And it has served
me very well."

Marian attended Catholic schools until the tenth grade. That's when she decided to switch to a local public school, which cultivated her passion for math and science. Marian thrived in that environment, which initiated her interest in science experiments. She rounded out her education by attending Princeton and the University of Southern California.

Marian holds a PhD in quantitative analysis (now data science) and social psychology.

"I finished my graduate studies on a
Friday," Marian said, "and I started
working at Bell Labs as a systems en-
gineer the following Monday. That was
in 1982, and I haven't stopped yet."

While at AT&T, Marian performed various functions related to network engineering, as well as voice and data communication. With the dawn of the internet, she shifted her focus to internet protocol technology. The AT&T brass gave her pushback. They didn't like the thought of replacing voice technology that routed phone calls over traditional telephone networks with internet routing. In time, Marian and her team were able to pull support for the shift to internet calls. AT&T then merged the voice and IP networking teams of around 2,000 individuals, with Marian at the head to create the new network. VoIP, the technology she helped create, has since been used to make text-based donations amounting to tens of millions of dollars. These digital donations were critical during several high-profile disasters, such as those caused by Hurricane Katrina and the 2010 earthquake in Haiti.

Marian held several senior positions with AT&T before leaving the company for Google, where she was hired as vice president of engineering. The mother of three adult children, Marian was inducted into the Women in Technology Hall of Fame in 2013. She continues to inspire creative minds and remains committed to expanding and improving technology. **U**

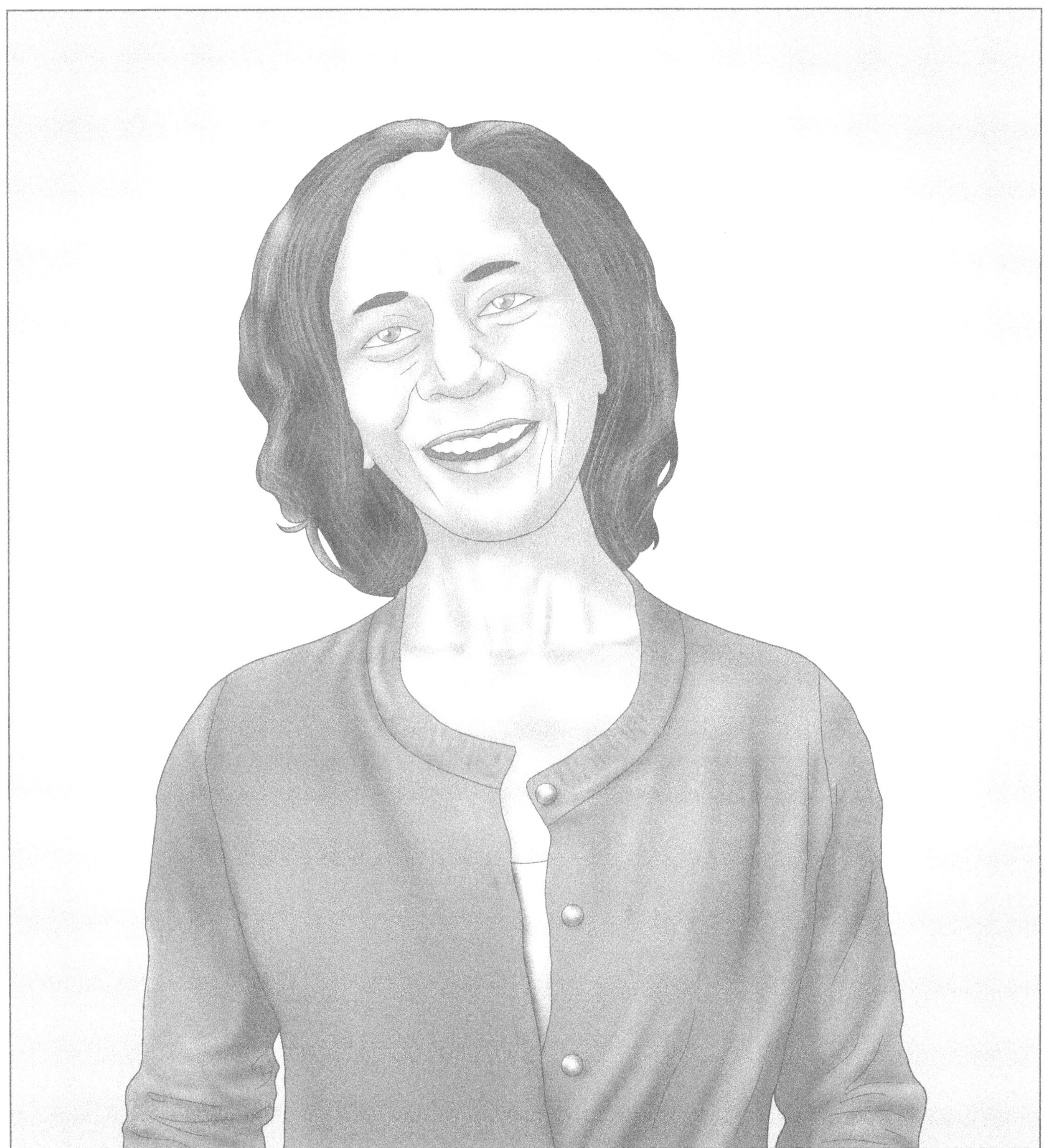

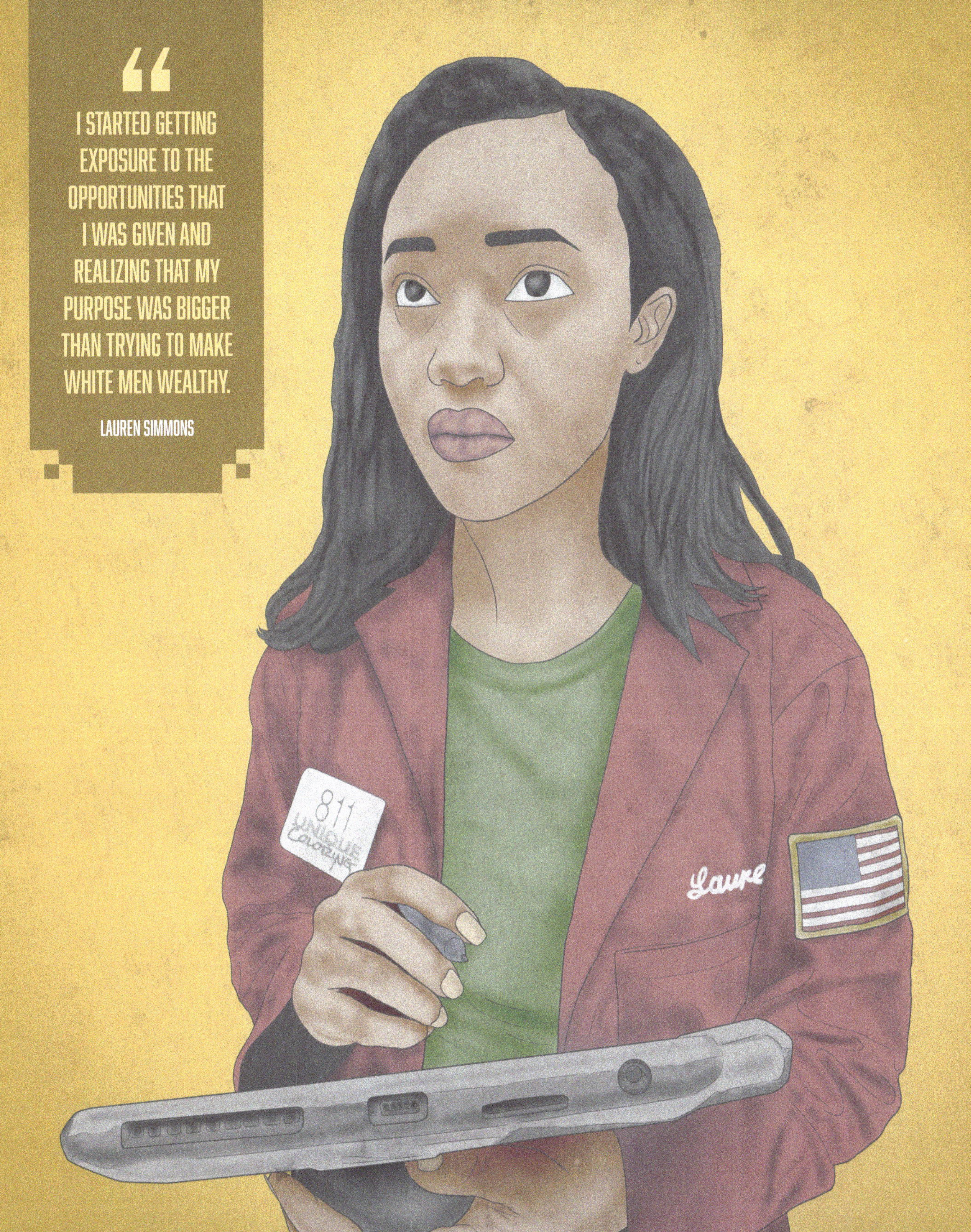

"
I STARTED GETTING EXPOSURE TO THE OPPORTUNITIES THAT I WAS GIVEN AND REALIZING THAT MY PURPOSE WAS BIGGER THAN TRYING TO MAKE WHITE MEN WEALTHY.
LAUREN SIMMONS
811
UNIQUE COLORING
Laure

LAUREN SIMMONS

At a mere 22-years old, Lauren Simmons stepped through the doors at 40 Wall Street and shattered a financial glass ceiling by becoming the youngest female trader on the floor of the New York Stock Exchange (NYSE). For a time, she was the only full-time female equity trader at NYSE. When word got out, she quickly became a media sensation, being featured on Fox, ABC, CNN, and CNBC, among several other outlets. After Gail Pankey-Albert, Lauren is the second black female trader in history to hold that position. But Lauren was something more—she was three things no one else has been at NYSE in a full-time capacity: a woman, a millennial, and a minority.

Lauren Simmons was born in Marietta, Georgia on August 11, 1994. She and her twin brother were raised by a single mother who instilled in them the importance of taking risks in pursuit of their dreams. Lauren attended a public research school, Kennesaw State University, not far from home. She originally wanted to be in architectural engineering, where she could design and build homes, but she wasn't selected for that program. That caused her to focus on genetics instead with the hope of establishing a career as a genetic counselor. In the process of writing her senior thesis, she found that it was going to be hard to advance in that chosen field. New York seemed to hold the answer to success. After graduating from Kennesaw State with a degree in genetics and a minor in statistics, she took a huge risk by flying to New York in December 2016 with no available career opportunities in place.

Once in New York, Lauren started applying for jobs. She relied on LinkedIn to set up face-to-face interviews with more than 300 senior staff at various companies, among them HR managers, CEOs, and other executives. This strategy caused her to stand out, and, while it led to a few interviews with people of influence, she was not hired. One criticism she received was related to her decision to switch career goals. Despite the rejections, Lauren—in an interview with Kiah McBride for Necole Kane—said:

> **"There was a reason why I had this gut feeling that I needed to be in New York. I didn't know what it was and what that was going to look like, but I knew I would find that job and I knew that it was going to work out."**

Undaunted, Lauren continued to send out her resume, and in a few months, someone who worked at a financial firm connected her with another person in equity. Before long, she was sitting with Gordon Charlop, a floor trader of 25 years and partner at a boutique trading firm called Rosenblatt Securities. Charlop was also a floor governor at NYSE, so he had the power to hire Lauren as an equity trader. But before she could become one, she was required to pass a notoriously difficult test for securities professionals. Lauren passed the test, and Charlop, who was impressed by her statistics background, hired the youngest female trader in NYSE history. While Lauren is no longer on the trading floor (she was only paid a paltry $12,000 per year after all), her signature remains in the constitution of the New York Stock Exchange. It was added on December 5, 2017, alongside legends like John D. Rockefeller. **U**

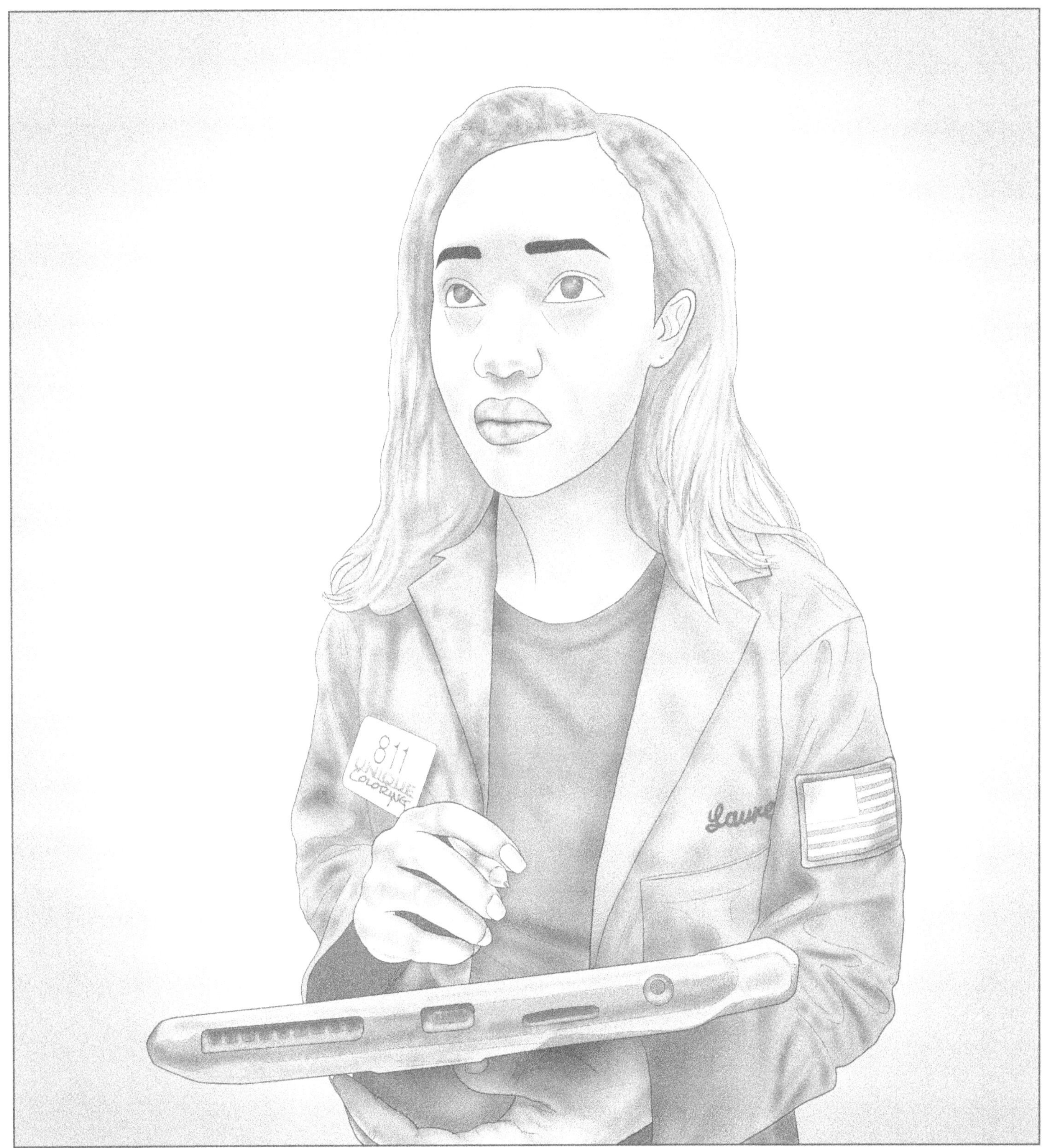

811
UNIQUE COLORING
Lauren

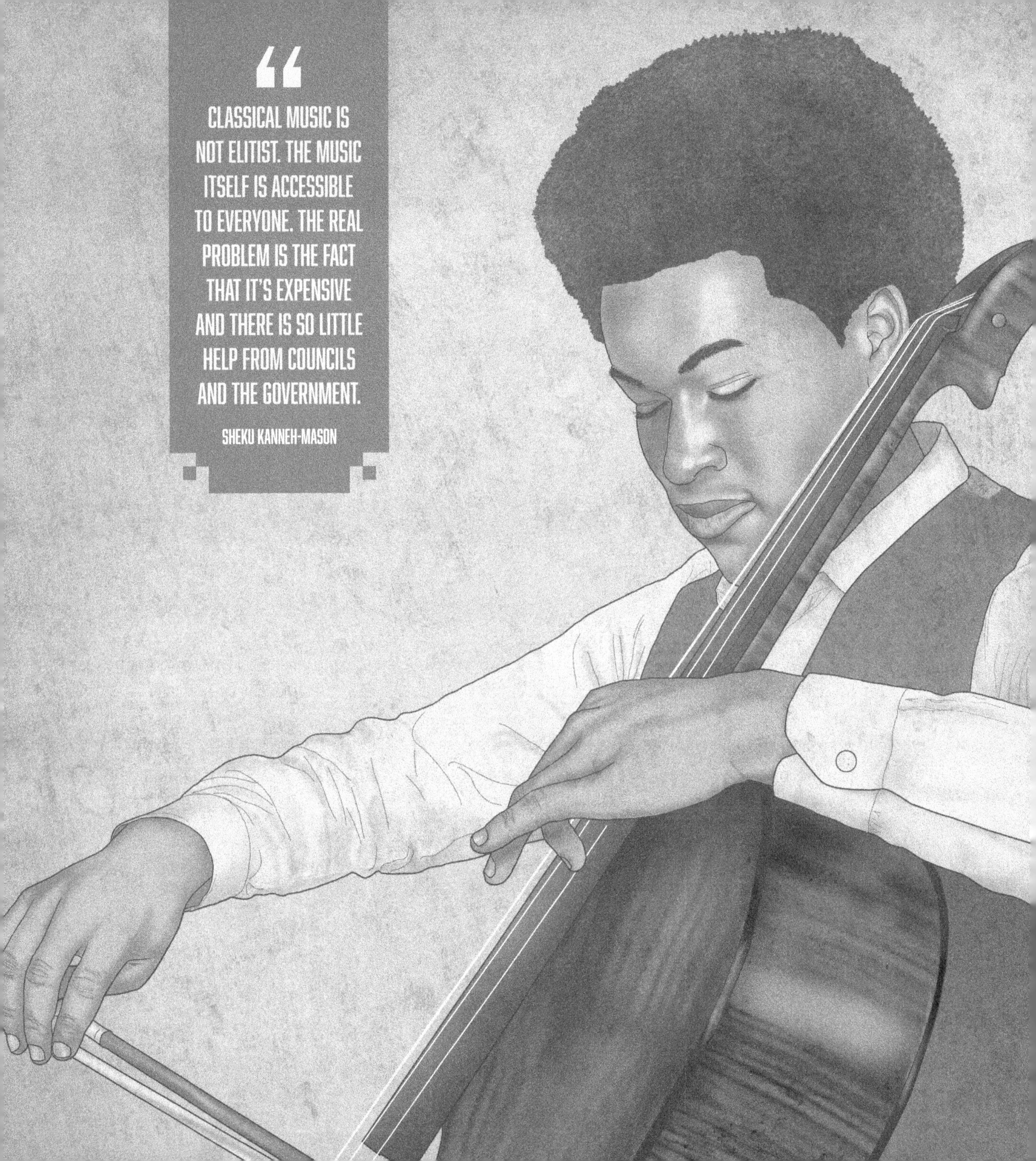
"
CLASSICAL MUSIC IS NOT ELITIST. THE MUSIC ITSELF IS ACCESSIBLE TO EVERYONE. THE REAL PROBLEM IS THE FACT THAT IT'S EXPENSIVE AND THERE IS SO LITTLE HELP FROM COUNCILS AND THE GOVERNMENT.
SHEKU KANNEH-MASON

SHEKU KANNEH-MASON

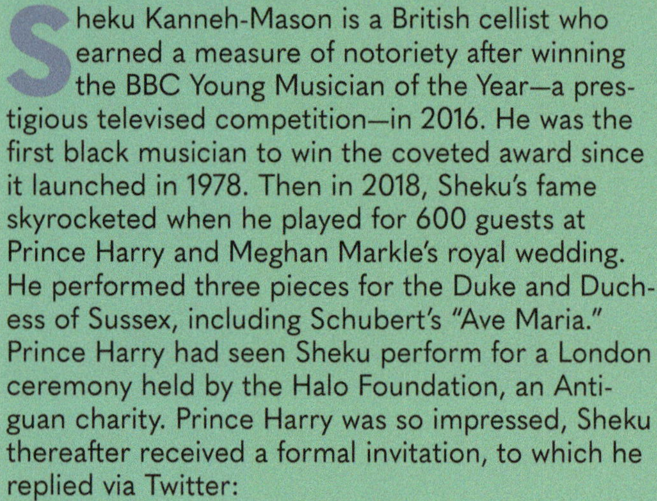

Sheku Kanneh-Mason is a British cellist who earned a measure of notoriety after winning the BBC Young Musician of the Year—a prestigious televised competition—in 2016. He was the first black musician to win the coveted award since it launched in 1978. Then in 2018, Sheku's fame skyrocketed when he played for 600 guests at Prince Harry and Meghan Markle's royal wedding. He performed three pieces for the Duke and Duchess of Sussex, including Schubert's "Ave Maria." Prince Harry had seen Sheku perform for a London ceremony held by the Halo Foundation, an Antiguan charity. Prince Harry was so impressed, Sheku thereafter received a formal invitation, to which he replied via Twitter:

"I was bowled over when Ms. Markle called me to ask if I would play during the ceremony and of course I immediately said yes!"

Since the wedding, Sheku went on to record albums for the British record label Decca Classics, all of which garnered acclaim. Sheku made history again in 2020 when his album *Elgar* landed in the Top 10 of the UK Official Album Chart, making him the first cellist to do so. Sheku has since toured the world and been on the cover of GQ. But during the heady moment of fame, he never lost focus on his studies as a full-time ABRSM Scholarship student at the Royal Academy of Music located in the heart of London.

Sheku Kanneh-Mason was born in a suburb of Nottingham, England on April 4, 1999. He is the third of seven children, all of whom are talented musicians. His parents are Stuart Mason, a senior vice president for the luxury hotel chain Belmond, and Dr. Kadiatu Kanneh-Mason, a former lecturer at Birmingham University. Sheku's eldest sister Isata was the first to express an interest in and aptitude for classical music. She played the piano well enough to be accepted into the Junior Department of the Royal Academy of Music at age eight. Following in Isata's footsteps, Sheku began his cello training at age six, under the guidance of Sarah Huson-Whyte. By age nine, he attended the Royal Academy on a junior scholarship as well and studied under Ben Davies in the Junior Department. He later studied with Hannah Roberts, the principal cellist of a chamber orchestra.

Sheku, along with his sister Isata and brother Braimah, joined the Chineke! Orchestra. Founded by double bass player Chi-chi Nwanoku, the orchestra caters to black and minority ethnic classical musicians, being the first of its kind in Europe. Sheku and his two siblings formed the Kanneh-Mason Trio and landed an appearance on Britain's Got Talent in 2015. The experience was a warm-up for Sheku's historic performance and win on BBC Young Musician. That win led to greater success, including his televised performance for the Royal Wedding—allegedly seen by billions—and his record deal with Decca Classics. His classical arrangement of Bob Marley's "No Woman No Cry" enjoyed 1 million streams on Spotify during its first month of release. His debut album *Inspiration* also became the first album of any winner of the Young Musician competition to chart in the UK. It entered the pop rankings at number 18, then re-entered at number 11 following the wedding performance. **U**

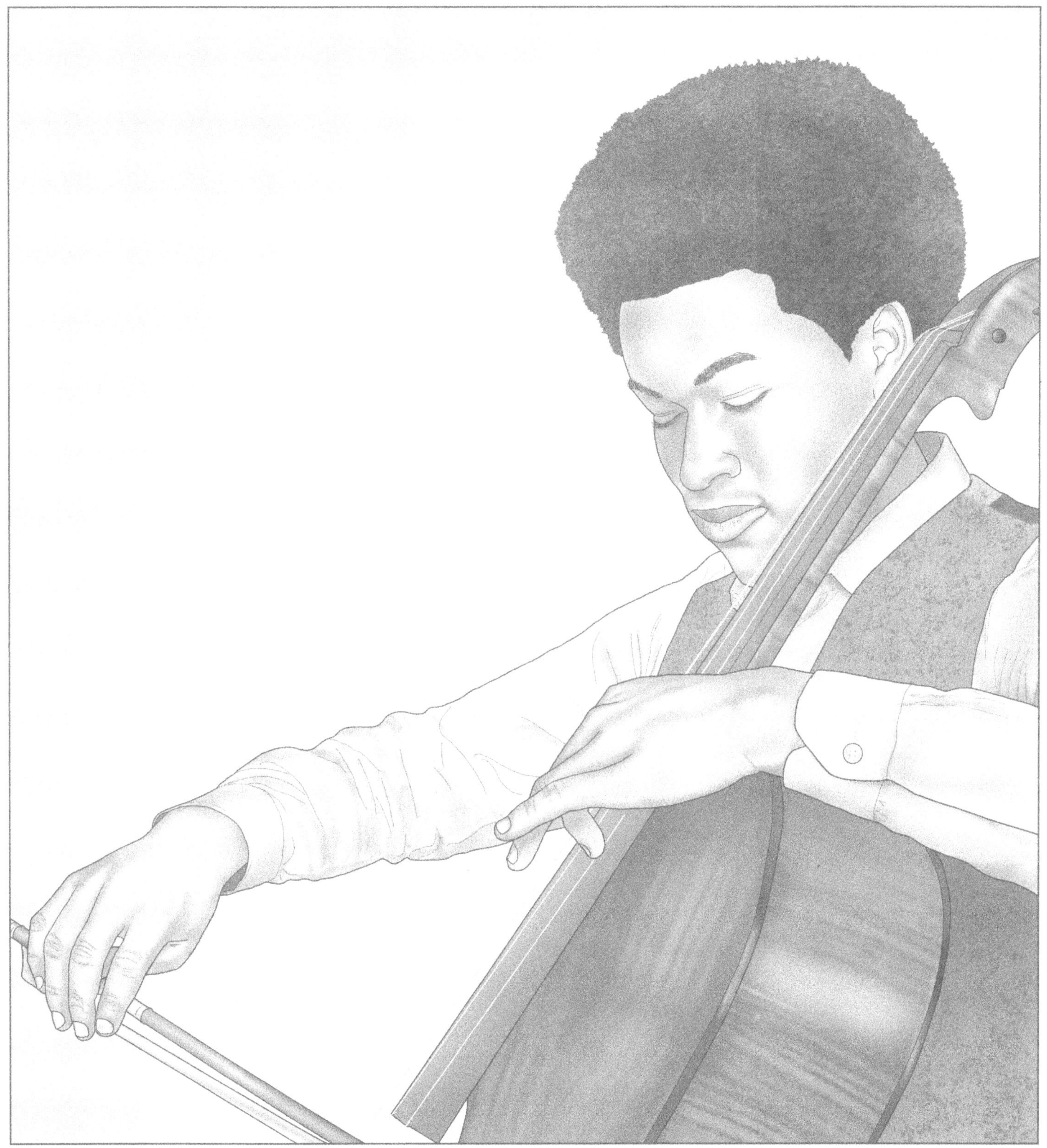

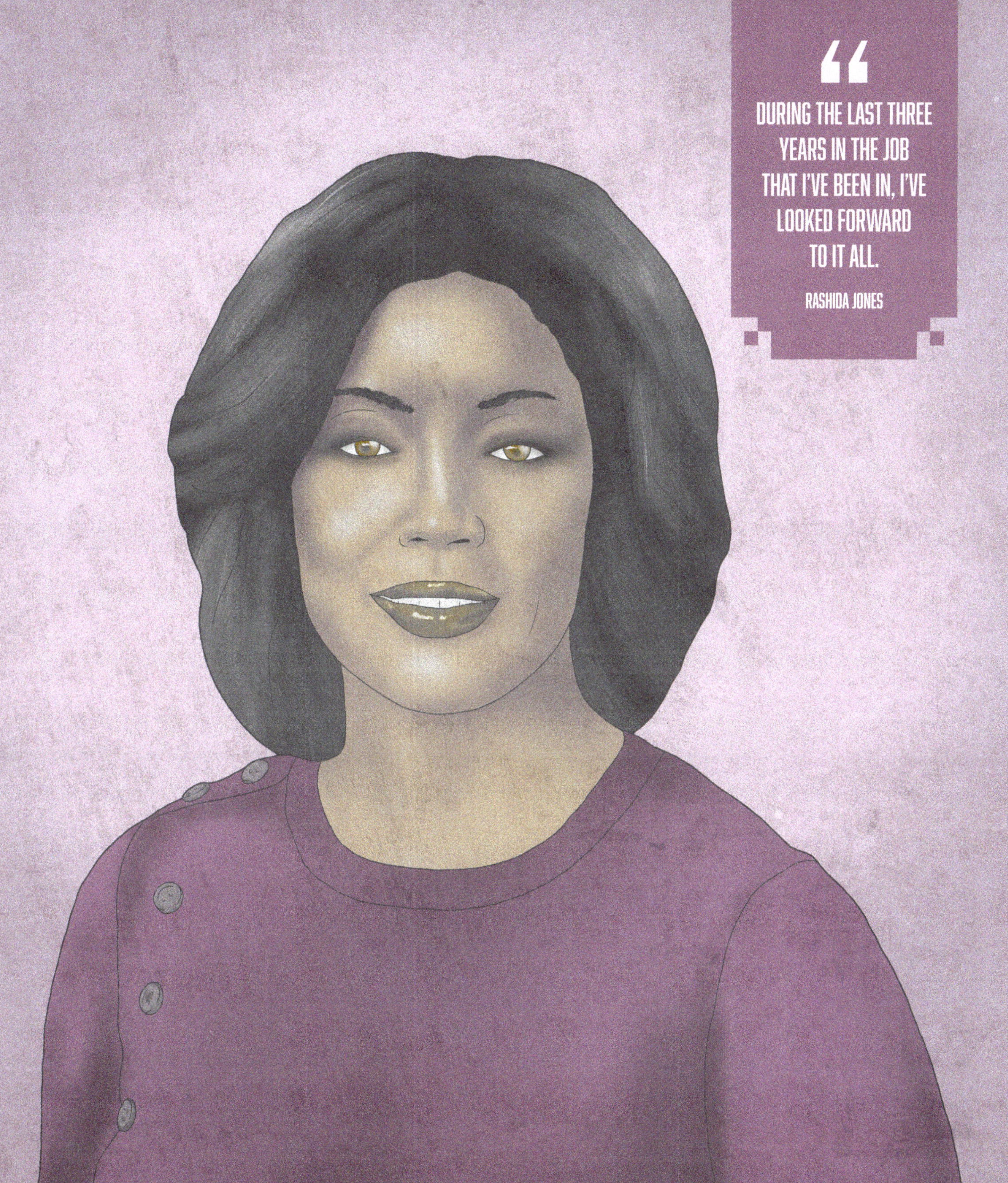
"
DURING THE LAST THREE
YEARS IN THE JOB
THAT I'VE BEEN IN, I'VE
LOOKED FORWARD
TO IT ALL.

RASHIDA JONES

RASHIDA JONES

On February 1, 2021, the first day of Black History Month, Rashida Jones, an MSNBC veteran, made history by stepping into the role of president of the cable news network. She is the first black person to hold that office. Rashida replaces Phil Griffin, who was president of MSNBC for twelve years and served in other capacities since MSNBC's inception in 1996. Being named network president at 40 years old is also a milestone for the black millennial, who amassed nearly two decades of experience working in the arenas of cable and local news.

In her role as executive producer, Rashida spearheaded news programs that delivered breaking news and covered major events for two networks, MSNBC and NBC News. She managed creative teams in producing content during election nights, political conventions, and Presidential Debates. She also determined the editorial focus of each show and directed the network-wide coverage related to COVID-19. In her previous role, she oversaw daytime and weekend programming as senior vice president of both NBC News and MSNBC. She is credited with overseeing the 2019 launch of the streaming network NBC News NOW, which allows the media giant to stay on the cutting edge. As president of MSNBC, her focus continues to be on the cable news network.

Rashida Jones was born on January 11, 1981, but she keeps her personal life private, so there is currently no available information about her childhood or marital status. She attended Henrico High School in Mecklenburg County, Virginia, and on the school's Facebook page, Rashida, when asked if she had a word for the folks back home, said:

"I often think back to walking the campus of Henrico High School where my teachers pushed me toward academic excellence and emboldened my passion to lead through my work. I have Henrico County Public Schools to thank for inspiring me to achieve goals beyond my dreams."

Rashida then attended Hampton University, from which she graduated in 2002 with a bachelor's in Mass Media Arts and Broadcast. While in college, she started her career in television news as a producer for the Norfolk, Virginia station WTKR-TV. While at the local station, she produced the 11 pm newscast and coordinated live coverage and weather reports. She transitioned to the Weather Channel in 2004 and remained there for a little over seven years. Rashida started as a producer at the Weather Channel, tasked with weekend primetime programming, and she moved through the ranks from senior producer to executive producer to director of live programming. NBC purchased the Weather Channel while she was in this senior role.

Greater responsibilities came after she moved to Columbia, South Carolina to work for the NBC-affiliate station WIS-TV. As news director, Rashida overhauled the news team, rebuilding and rebranding it to achieve more in-depth investigative reporting. Under her leadership, WIS-TV was the number one station in Columbia, South Carolina. Her time at MSNBC and NBC News began in August of 2013, and her journey from executive producer to president of the entire network was underway. U

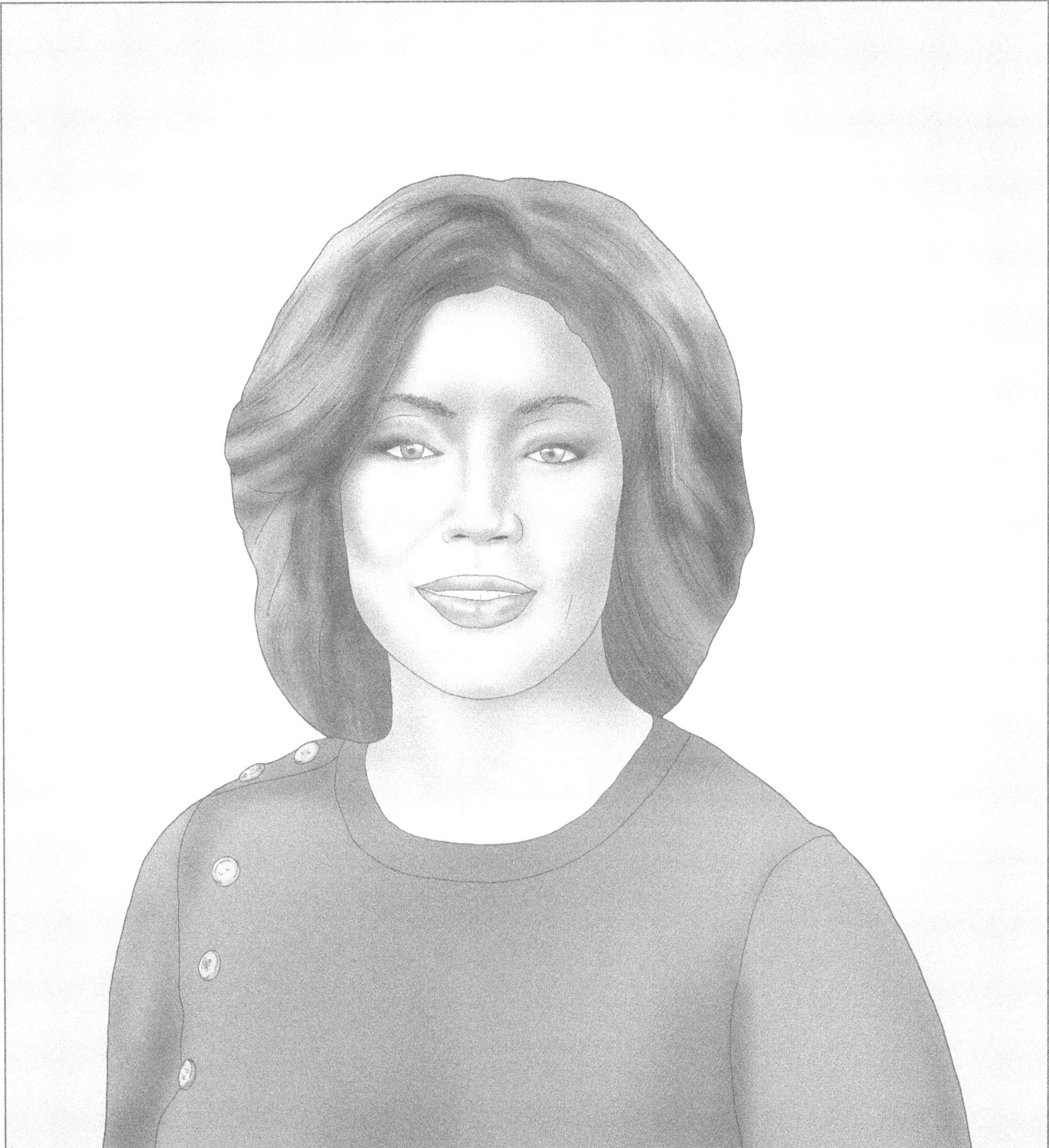

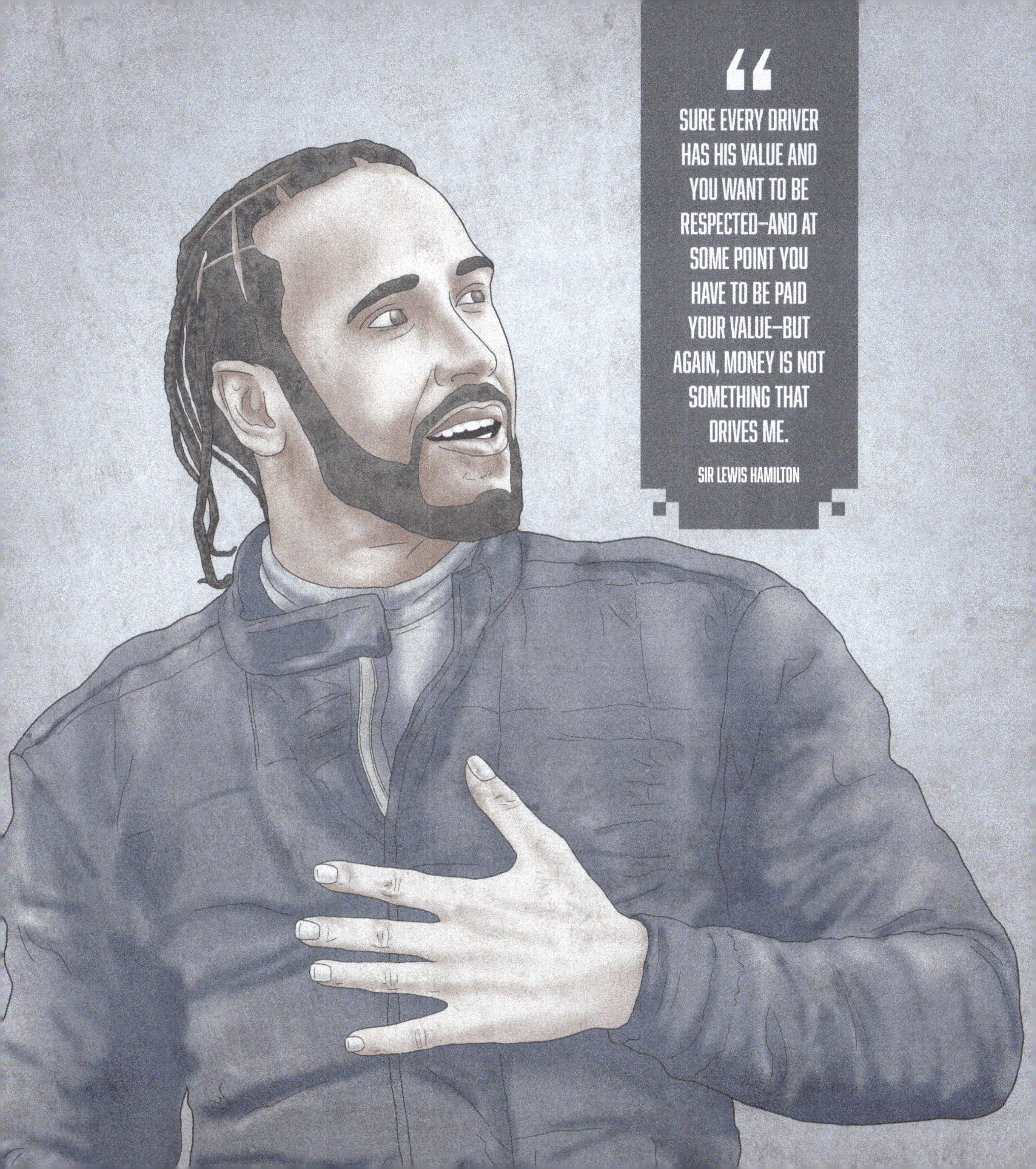

"
SURE EVERY DRIVER HAS HIS VALUE AND YOU WANT TO BE RESPECTED—AND AT SOME POINT YOU HAVE TO BE PAID YOUR VALUE—BUT AGAIN, MONEY IS NOT SOMETHING THAT DRIVES ME.
SIR LEWIS HAMILTON

SIR LEWIS HAMILTON

Sir Lewis Hamilton is a British race-car driver who has won the most Formula One (F1) races and holds more pole positions and podium finishes than any other F1 driver in the history of the sport. He is noted for winning seven world titles, a record that currently ties him with F1 legend Michael Schumacher. Lewis made history in 2008 when he became the first black F1 driver to win the World Drivers' Championship.

Lewis Carl Davidson Hamilton was born on January 7, 1985, in Stevenage, Hertfordshire, England. His father, a black man named Anthony Hamilton, hails from the island of Grenada, while his mother, Carmen Larbalestier, is white. Yet Lewis identifies as black, as stated in his 2014 interview with the BBC:

"When I first started in Formula 1, I tried to ignore the fact I was the first black guy ever to race in the sport. But, as I've got older, I've really started to appreciate the implications. It's a pretty cool feeling to be the person to knock down a barrier."

When Lewis was five, his father Anthony bought him a remote-controlled (RC) car, which sparked his fascination with autos. A year later, Lewis was runner-up in a British RC racing championship. Lewis officially started his racing career at the tender age of eight mainly with the help of his father, who worked several odd jobs to support his karting endeavors. Two years later, he won the British cadet karting championship, a racing event several famous drivers entered and won before launching their adult race car driving careers.

Lewis went on to win other karting competitions over the next two years as well, and by age 15, he was the youngest driver to be ranked number one in competitive karting. But the year he first won the British karting championship, he went to the Autosport Awards and approached Ron Dennis, the boss of the McLaren Formula One team. After asking for an autograph he told Ron Dennis of his British karting win and said he wanted to race his cars one day. In 1998, after Lewis had won two more important championships, Ron Dennis called to offer him a spot in the McLaren and Mercedes-Benz Young Driver Support program. Lewis signed on, and there he received the resources and training needed to improve his driving skills.

He accomplished another first with the contract signing because being 13 years of age made him the youngest driver ever contracted by an F1 team. The contract also included a future option, exclusive to team members, that allowed entry into Formula One. Lewis raced at the Junior Intercontinental A level for a time, then graduated to Formula Renault, an entry-level motor racing series popular in Europe and other areas. After a slow start in Formula Renault, Lewis raced to the top with a series of impressive wins that included fastest laps and a bounty of points. A stint in Formula 3 (F3) followed, F3 being a third-tier class of open-wheel formula racing. Then came the GP2 Series, another form of open-wheel racing that is the natural progression to Formula 1. Indeed, Lewis Hamilton's rookie performance in F1, which took place in 2007, is considered among the greatest in the sport. He eventually rose to the top of the all-time pole positions list and matched Michael Schumacher by winning seven world titles. **U**

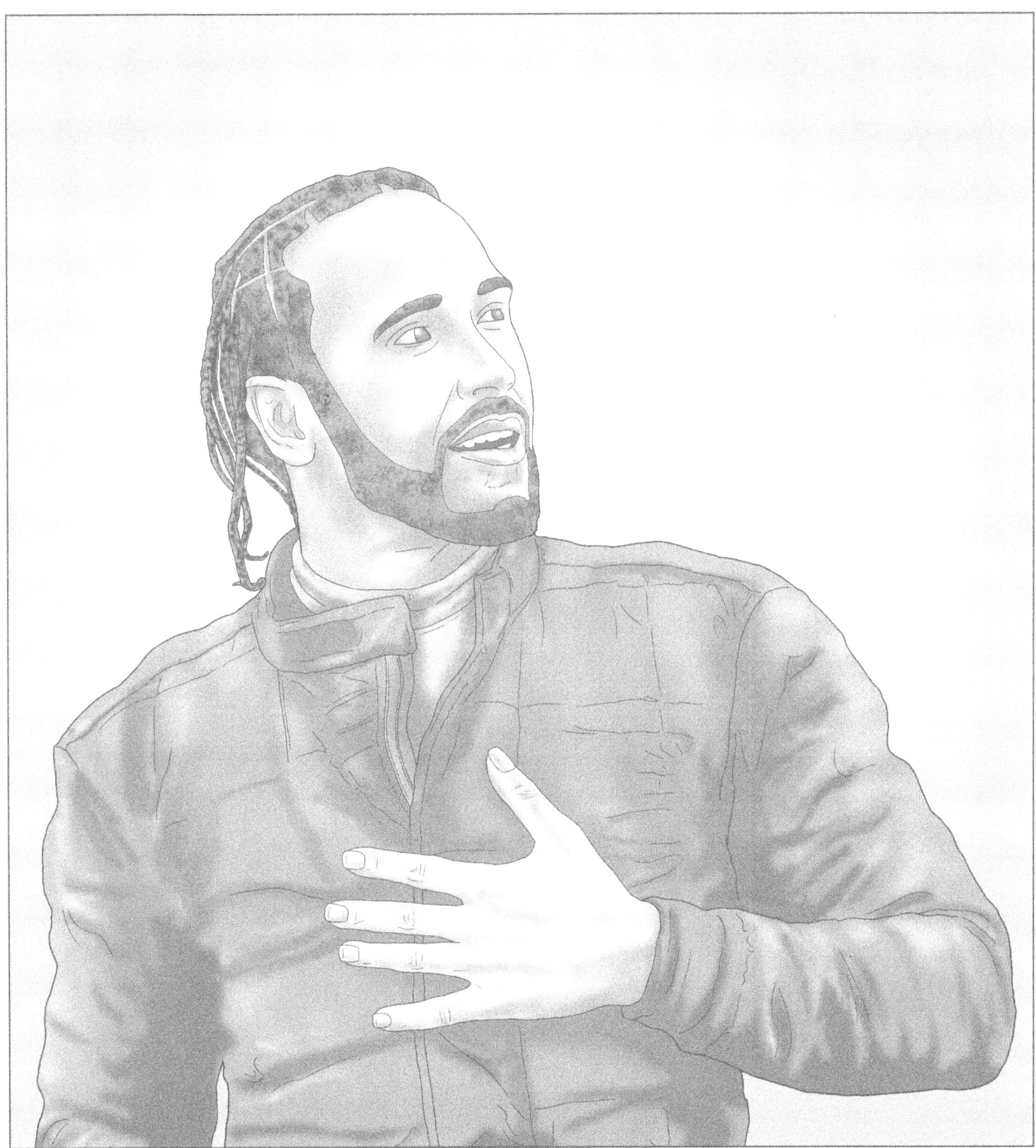

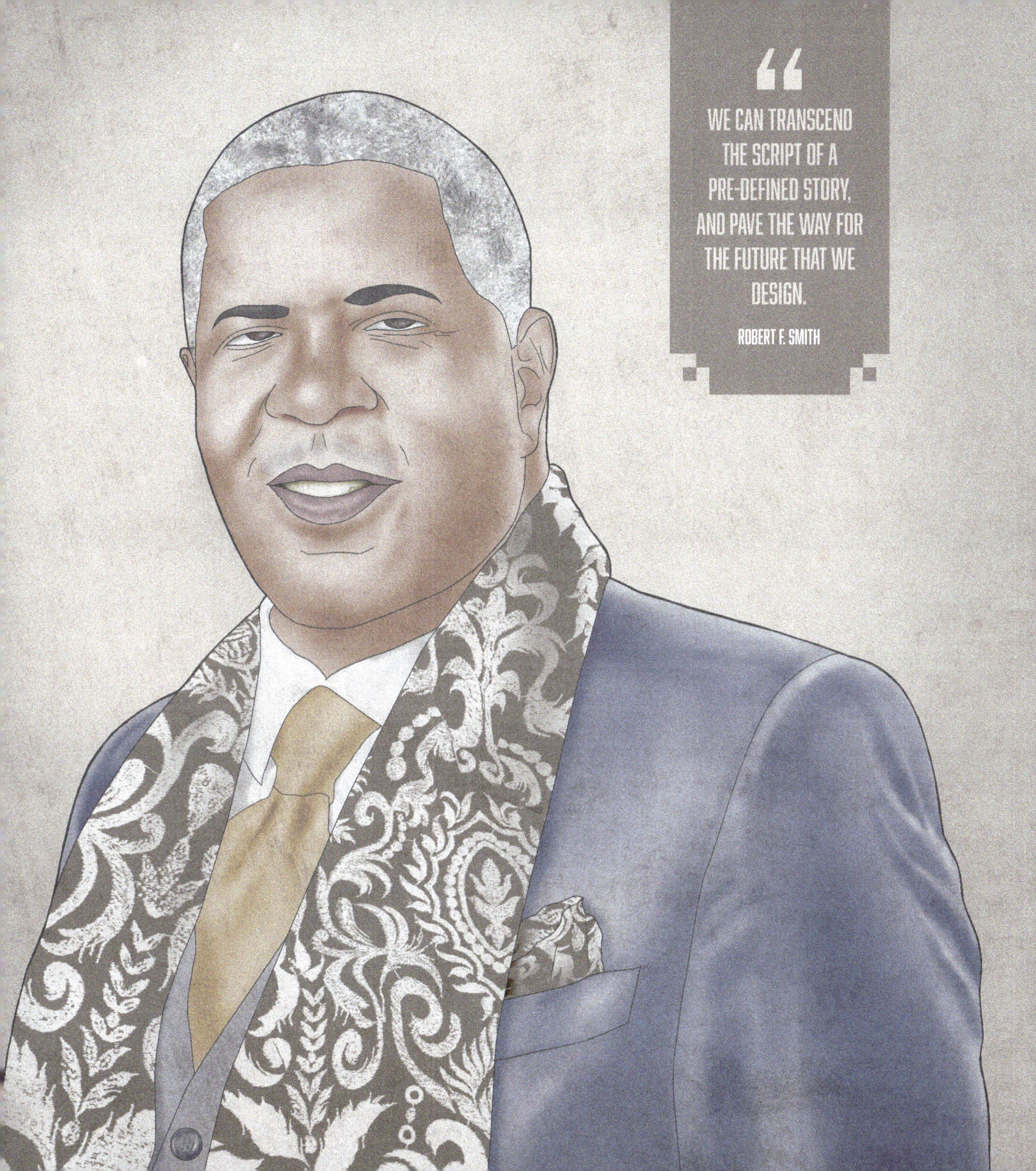
WE CAN TRANSCEND
THE SCRIPT OF A
PRE-DEFINED STORY,
AND PAVE THE WAY FOR
THE FUTURE THAT WE
DESIGN.
ROBERT F. SMITH

ROBERT F. SMITH

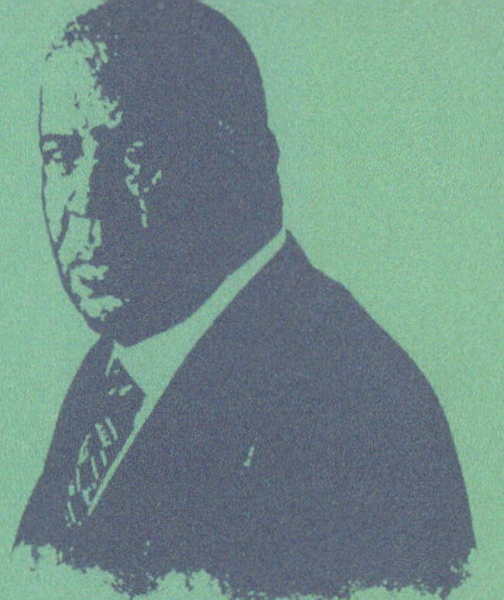

Robert F. Smith, a black billionaire from Colorado, is the founder, chairman, and CEO of the private equity firm Vista Equity Partners. Established in 2000, Vista Equity exclusively invests in business software startup ventures, which it buys and manages more efficiently to handily increase their value. Vista Equity Partners manages over $73 billion in assets and has amassed a personal net worth for Smith to the tune of $7.05 billion as of this writing. That means his net worth has tripled since 2016. His company is among the best-performing private equity firms in the space and, since its founding, posted annualized returns of 22% according to *Forbes*.

But aside from his private equity investments, Smith is also known for his philanthropy. He is a generous giver, and that fact was cemented in May of 2019 during a commencement speech he gave at Morehouse College in Atlanta, Georgia. Smith promised to pay off the collective student loans of that year's graduating class, which he later extended to include the parents of the graduates. The gift, according to Moorehouse officials, totaled $34 million. Smith also received an honorary doctorate from the historically black college.

Robert Frederick Smith was born in Denver, Colorado on December 1, 1962. His parents, Dr. William Robert Smith and Dr. Sylvia Myrna Smith were both teachers who enjoyed a middle-class status. Smith found the number for Bell Labs Innovations and applied for an internship while attending Denver East High School, but was denied. During a 2015 commencement address at the American University School of International Service, Smith added:

"They said I could apply if I were a junior or senior in college. I said that was fantastic, because, while I was only a junior in high school, I was getting A's in computer science and my advanced math courses, so it was like I was in college. Much to my dismay, they disagreed."

Smith continued to call Bell Labs every day for the next two weeks, then each Monday for several months, until a position opened up after an M.I.T. student did not attend. That summer Smith developed a reliability test for semiconductors, an invention that won him praise from fellow interns as well as supervisors. He continued to intern for Bell Labs in the summers and during winter breaks while attending Cornell University in Ithaca, New York. He graduated from the prestigious university in 1985 and received an engineering degree. Cornell's School of Chemical and Biomolecular Engineering was named after Smith following a hefty $50 million donation, and in 2020, they also favored him with their highest honor, the Distinguished Alumni Award.

He worked as a chemical engineer for a few years and even received European and U.S. patents for two inventions, but investment banking seemed to be his calling. Smith made the transition in 1994 when he accepted a job at Goldman Sachs in the technology investment banking department. In 2000, Smith left Goldman Sachs to establish his own private equity and venture capital firm, which is now the fourth-largest enterprise software company in the world behind Microsoft, Oracle, and SAP. U

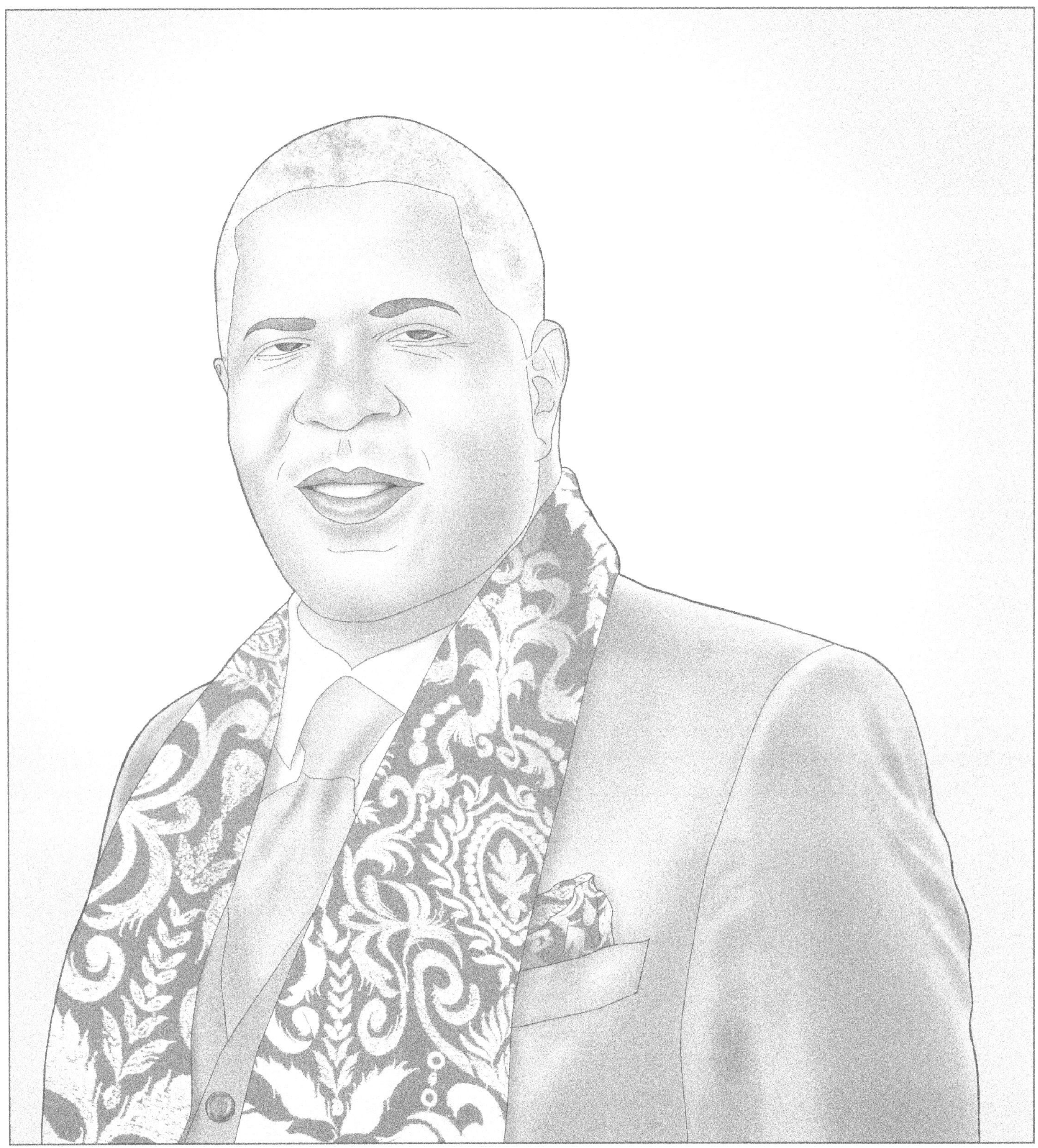

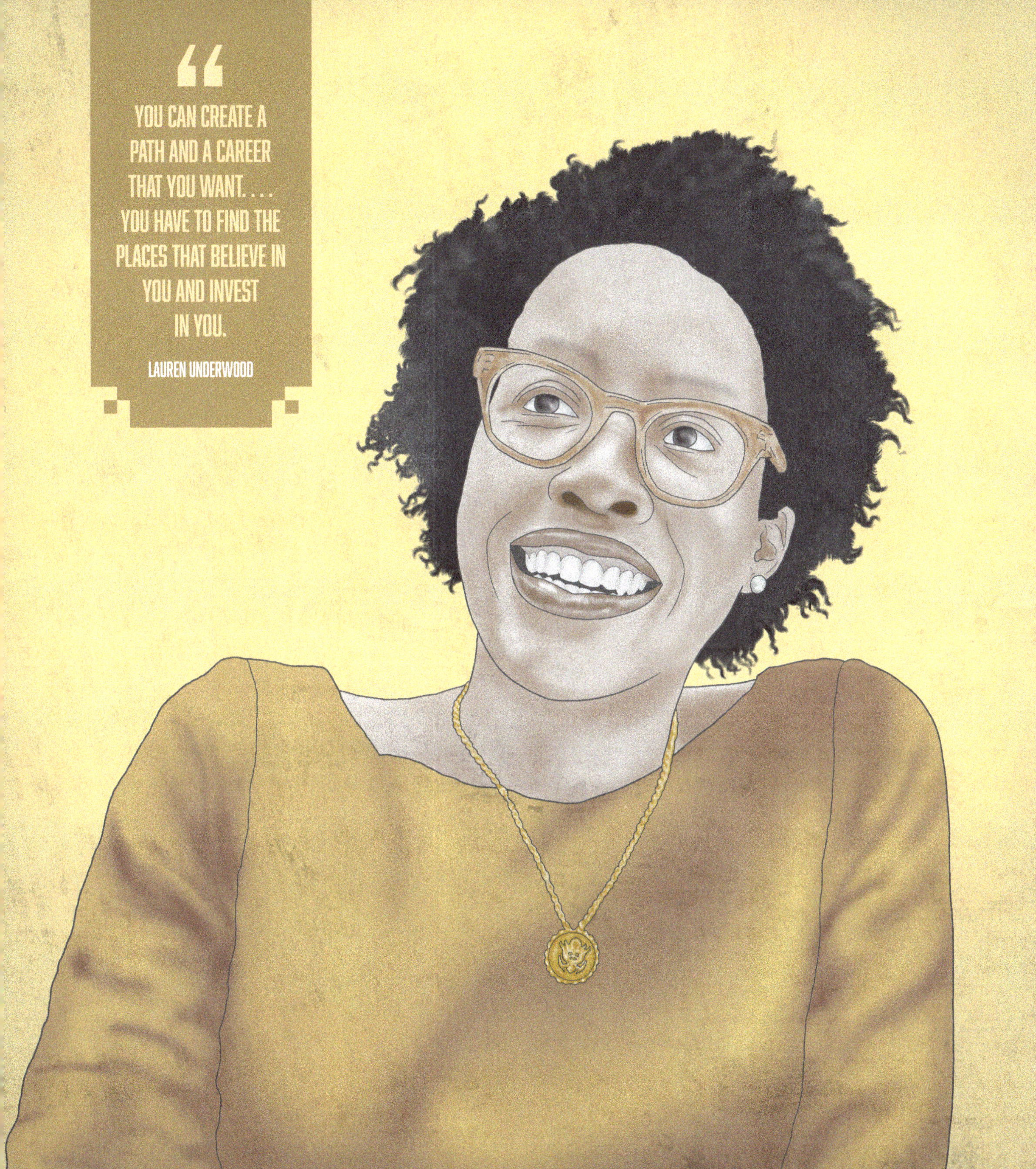
"
YOU CAN CREATE A
PATH AND A CAREER
THAT YOU WANT. . . .
YOU HAVE TO FIND THE
PLACES THAT BELIEVE IN
YOU AND INVEST
IN YOU.

LAUREN UNDERWOOD

LAUREN UNDERWOOD

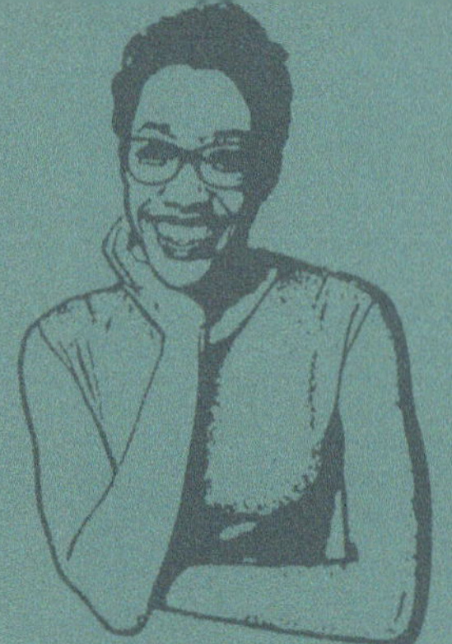

Lauren Underwood, a Naperville, Illinois resident, made history on Thursday, January 3, 2019, by being the youngest black woman to be sworn in to the U.S. House of Representatives. At only 32 years of age, Underwood became a member of the 116th Congress, representing Illinois' 14th Congressional District. For Naperville itself, where she is from, Underwood made other historic firsts: she was the first millennial and the first black person of either sex to represent her community in Congress. In a press release issued one week later, Underwood said:

"It is a new day in the House of Representatives. In the Democratic Majority, when the American people have elected the most diverse Congress with more women serving than ever before, we are demonstrating a commitment to conducting the business of our Nation with the highest standards of ethics and decency."

The swearing-in ceremony was occasioned by the passage of the Opening Day Rules package, which included a pair of provisions to the Congressional Accountability Act. The provisions, which Underwood wrote, prohibit members of Congress and their committee staff from establishing sexual relationships. And they also prohibit the issuance of non-disclosure agreements to silence victims of sexual assault and those who witness such assaults.

Lauren Ashley Underwood was born in Mayfield Heights, Ohio, on October 4, 1986. She and her family moved to Naperville, Illinois, when she was three. Underwood became a Girl Scout in kindergarten and is a lifetime member. She graduated from Neuqua Valley High School in 2004. While a junior in high school, she served on the City of Naperville's Fair Housing Advisory Commission, then she attended the University of Michigan, where, in 2008, she earned a Bachelor of Science in Nursing.

During her first year in nursing school, Underwood was drawn to politics after taking a course on policy and politics in nursing and healthcare. She later earned two master's degrees in public health nursing from John Hopkins University. She began a career as a registered nurse in 2008, during which she attended university and worked as a policy coordinator for the U.S. Department of Health and Human Services (HHS). She later rose to special assistant/senior advisor for HHS and helped to implement the Affordable Care Act. She also served as an adjunct instructor, teaching future nurses via Georgetown University's online master's program.

Underwood announced her candidacy for the U.S. House of Representatives in August of 2017. She ran on a platform that focused on affordable healthcare. In her first run for office, Underwood went on to defeat six men in the primary, and with the endorsement of former President Barack Obama and Vice President Joe Biden, she successfully unseated incumbent Republican Randy Hultgren in the general election. In her first term, she wrote six bills that were signed into law, including one that lowered the cost of diabetes medication. Underwood secured a second term in the November 2020 election, narrowly defeating State Senator Jim Oberweis. Ⓤ

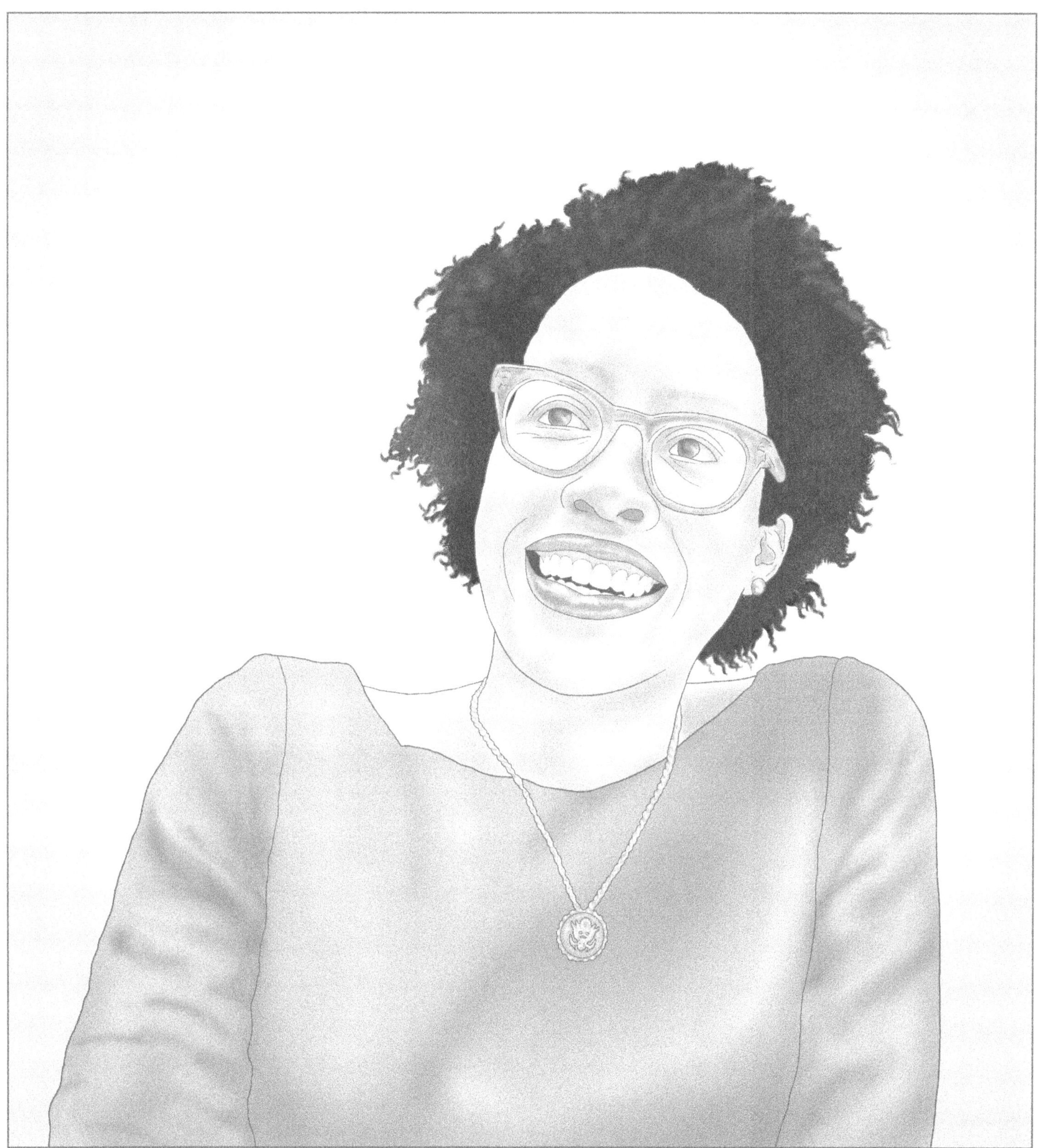

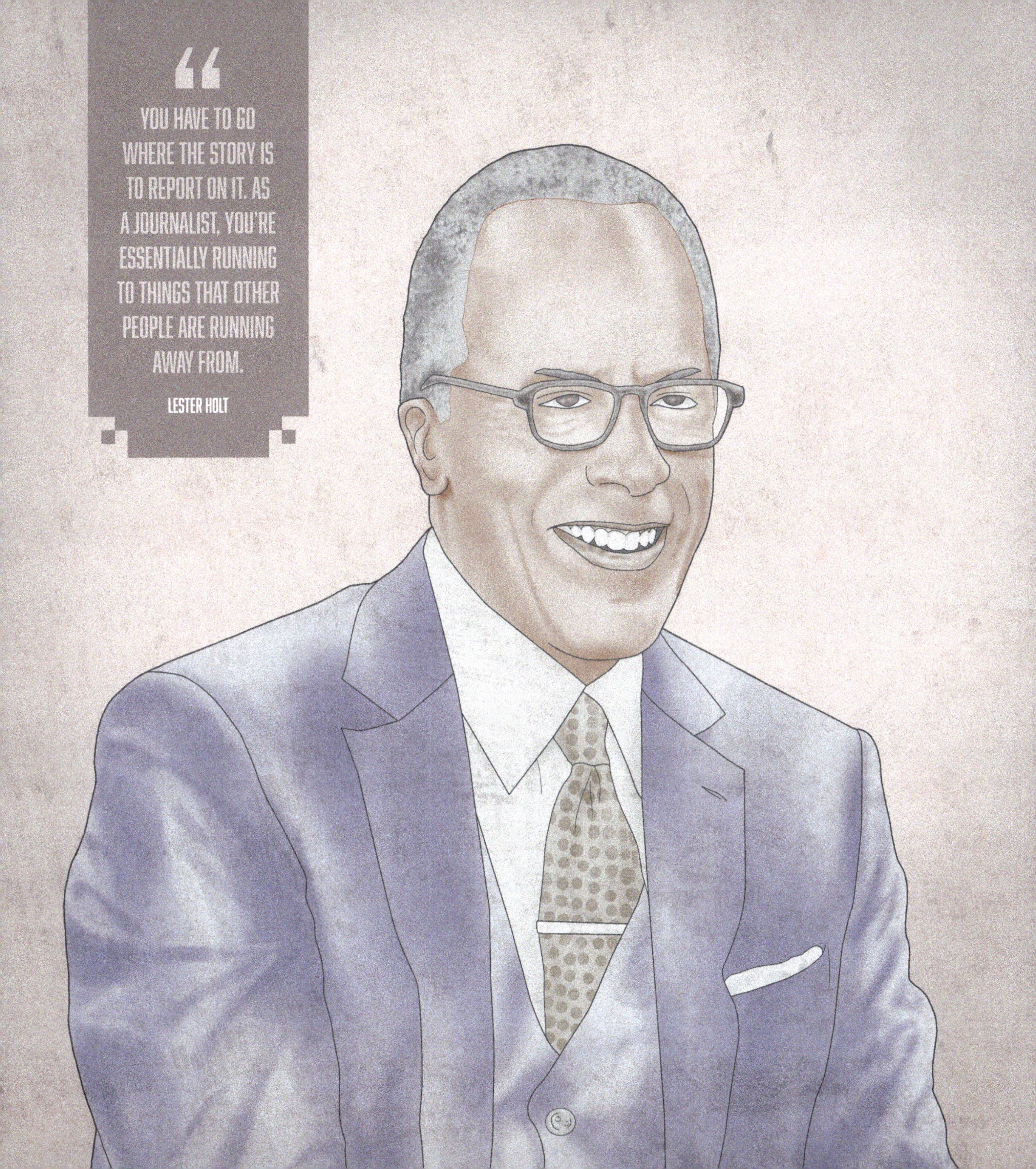
"
YOU HAVE TO GO
WHERE THE STORY IS
TO REPORT ON IT. AS
A JOURNALIST, YOU'RE
ESSENTIALLY RUNNING
TO THINGS THAT OTHER
PEOPLE ARE RUNNING
AWAY FROM.
LESTER HOLT

LESTER HOLT

Award-winning journalist Lester Holt rose through the ranks in a four-decade career that landed him in the seat of a flagship newscast for NBC that ranked number one in America under former hosts Tom Brokaw and Brian Williams. Since September 2011, Holt has served as principal anchor of the signature newsmagazine "Dateline NBC." He was also named the "most trusted television news personality in America" by a 2018 *Hollywood Reporter*/Morning Consult poll.

Lester Don Holt, Jr. was born on Hamilton Air Force Base in Marin County, California on March 8, 1959. He is the youngest of four children, and his parents, Lester Don Holt, Sr. and June (DeRozario) Holt are both of Jamaican descent. Holt grew up in Rancho Cordova, a city in Sacramento County, California. While in high school, Holt applied to several companies for work, but two months after graduating from Cordova High School in 1977, he received a rejection letter from NBC. Holt's first paying broadcast job did come, but not in the way he expected. In a February 2012 issue of *American Profile* magazine, Holt said:

> "My first on-air job was actually as a disc jockey at a Country and Western station. The only time I could land a full-time gig was if I was willing to re-port the news."

He worked at the radio station on weekends while attending California State University in Sac-ramento, where he majored in government, but he dropped out in 1979 after the station offered him a full-time job, which obligated him to report the news. Talking to late-night host Seth Meyers, Holt added:

> "They put me in a Jeep Cherokee with police scanners and two-way radios and I hit the streets and start-ed covering news and I never looked back."

CBS was the first major network to give Holt a shot at the career he was aiming for, when, In 1981, he landed a job at the television station in New York. He left New York to work at local CBS stations in Los Angeles and Chicago, but by 1983 he was back in New York working for CBS as a reporter and weekend anchor. Holt moved to Chicago-based WBBM-TV in 1986 and spent the next 14 years anchoring the evening news. But in 2000, the year he joined NBC, he was demoted from his anchor position, which devastated him for a time.

Despite the blow, Holt applied to MSNBC for an anchor position, which resulted in the daily news show, *Lester Holt Live*. He also served as MSNBC's primary anchor, which involved coverage of the network's major news events. In 2003 he moved to NBC News and was made a substitute anchor for *NBC Nightly News* and *Today*. When Brian Williams, host of *NBC Nightly News* took medical leave in 2013 for knee surgery, Holt took over hosting duties for the broadcast. Then in 2015, Brian Williams was suspended for exaggerating a story about being aboard a U.S. military helicopter in Iraq that drew enemy fire. After serving as the interim anchor for a few months, Holt became the permanent *NBC Nightly News* anchor in June of that year. **U**

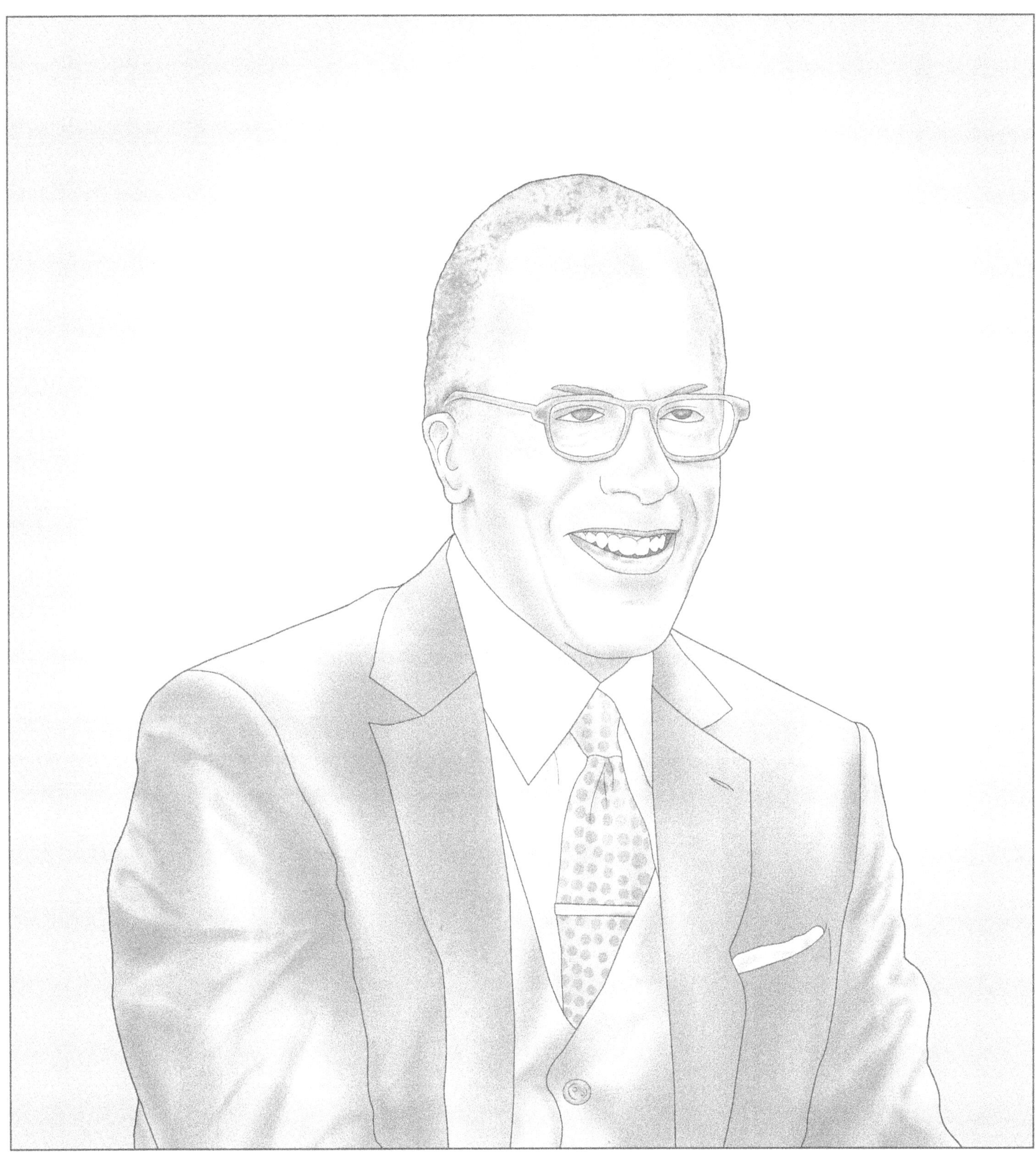

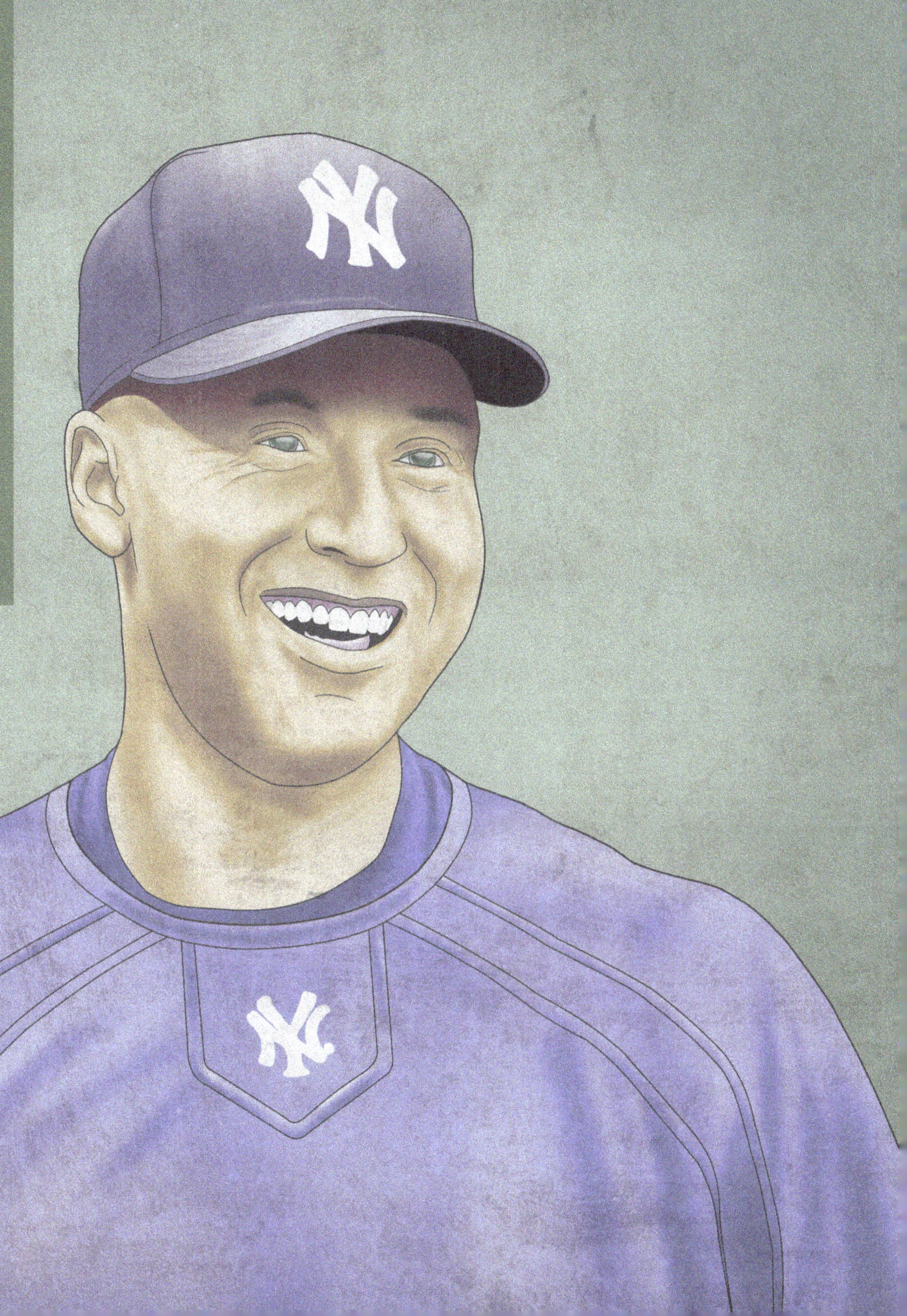
YOU HEAR PEOPLE LAUGH AT YOU AND TELL YOU TO PUT REAL THINGS, REAL THOUGHTS IN YOUR HEAD. AND NO ONE FROM KALAMAZOO, MICHIGAN, IS GOING TO BE ABLE TO PLAY FOR THE NEW YORK YANKEES, BUT I USED THAT AS MOTIVATION.
DEREK JETER

DEREK JETER

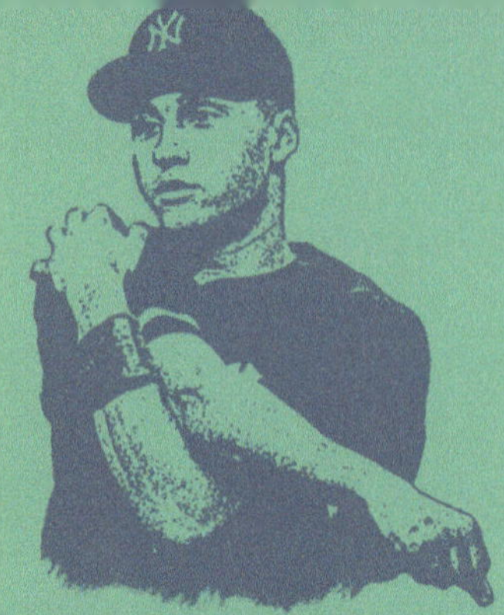

A five-time World Series champion, Derek Jeter spent his 20-year career in Major League Baseball with the same team: the New York Yankees. During that time, he won awards for the best overall hitter and best-fielding shortstop in the league. In his prime, Jeter was considered one of the greatest hitters in the sport, and the 11 seasons he batted over .300 was proof of that. In 2009, Jeter made history with his record-breaking 2,674th career hit, the most made by a shortstop in the majors. Then in 2011, he became only the 28th player to register 3,000 career hits.

Major League Baseball is among the hardest sports in which a player can enter the Hall of Fame. Since 1876, the year the National League started, close to 20,000 men have dawned a Major League uniform, as of this writing. Of that number, only 333 hang in the National Baseball Hall of Fame and Museum in Cooperstown, New York. That is a scant 1.67% of all the executives, pioneers, managers, umpires, and players who participated in the sport. Yet Derek Jeter, a Yankees icon and captain, received a nearly unanimous election to the Hall of Fame in 2020. Of the 397 ballots submitted, his name was on all but one. Only Mariano Rivera, the one player to be elected unanimously to the Hall of Fame, fared better than Jeter.

Derek Sanderson Jeter was born on June 26, 1974, in Pequannock, New Jersey. His mother, a white woman of English, Irish, and German ancestry named Dorothy, was an accountant. His father, Sanderson Charles Jeter—a black American who held a PhD—was a substance abuse counselor. His parents met while stationed in Germany, as they both served in the U.S. Army. Consequently, Jeter's father, Sanderson, was a standout shortstop on the baseball team at Fisk University in Nashville, Tennessee. No wonder then, that Jeter had his sights set on becoming a professional baseball player.

Jeter got an early start in the sport, playing Little League at around age five, after the family moved to Kalamazoo, Michigan. Jeter and his younger sister often spent the summer in New Jersey with their grandparents. It was those summers when his grandparents stayed up at night to watch the New York Yankees play on TV that made Jeter a fan of the team. One of his favorite players at the time was outfielder Dave Winfield. When speaking with Karl Ravech of ESPN, Jeter said:

"Obviously, the pinstripes stood out first and foremost. I think when you're young, it's a visual love affair. And it was [Dave] Winfield. Big Dave was my guy, you know. I thought he was larger than life…. We used to watch all the highlights. So, I tried to learn as much as I could about the past Yankee teams, and I just couldn't think of a better organization to play for."

After retiring in 2014, Jeter focused on business. He launched an online media company called The Players' Tribune and a publishing imprint with Simon & Schuster called Jeter Publishing. But, most notably, in 2017, Jeter and a group of investors purchased the Miami Marlins for $1.2 billion. He was named CEO, and the purchase makes him the first black person to own a Major League team. U

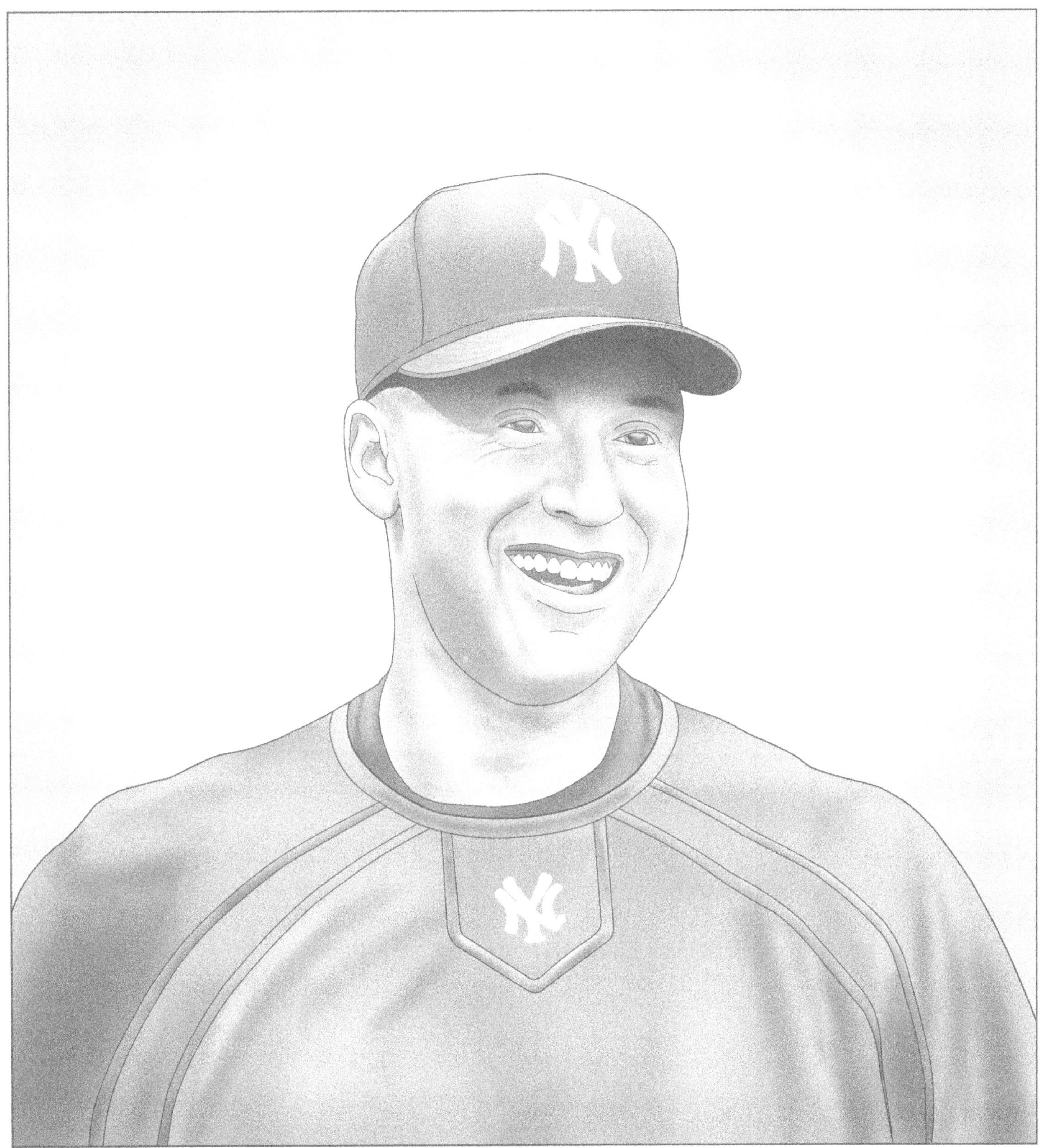

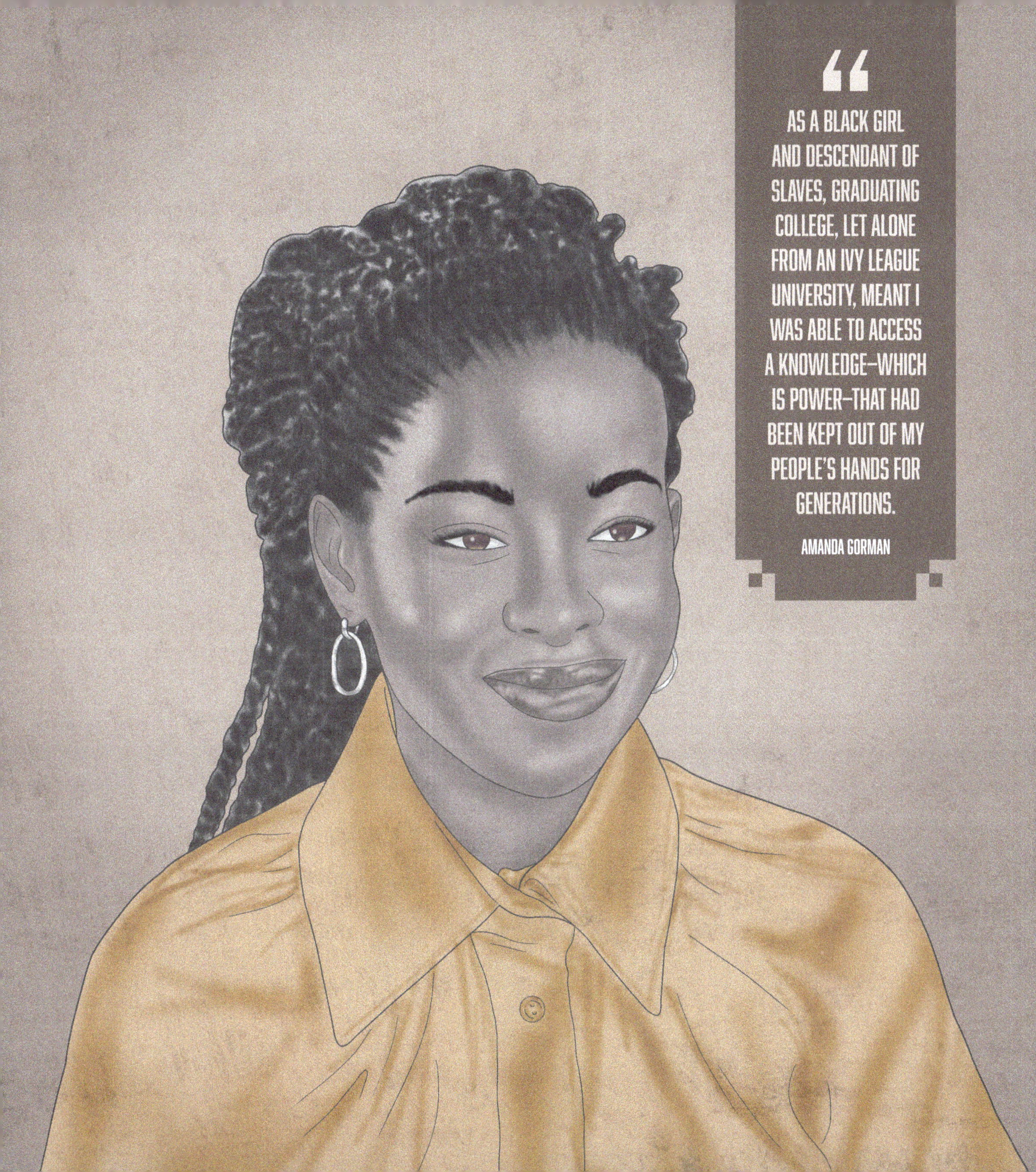

AS A BLACK GIRL
AND DESCENDANT OF
SLAVES, GRADUATING
COLLEGE, LET ALONE
FROM AN IVY LEAGUE
UNIVERSITY, MEANT I
WAS ABLE TO ACCESS
A KNOWLEDGE—WHICH
IS POWER—THAT HAD
BEEN KEPT OUT OF MY
PEOPLE'S HANDS FOR
GENERATIONS.

AMANDA GORMAN

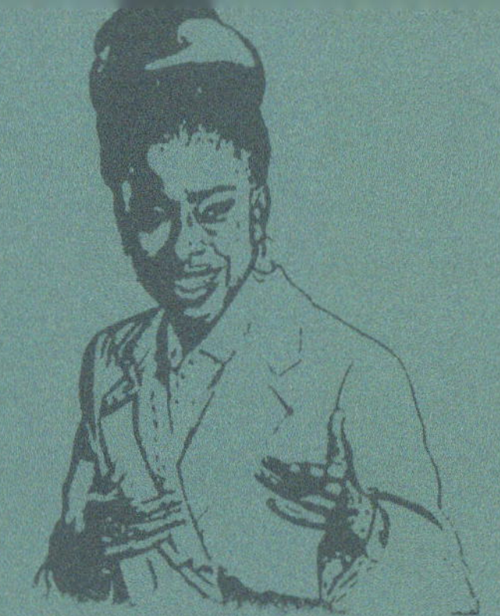

AMANDA GORMAN

At a mere 22 years old, Amanda Gorman became the youngest inaugural poet in history when she was chosen by an inaugural committee to recite "The Hill We Climb" on January 20, 2021, during President Joe Biden's swearing-in ceremony. But Amanda is no stranger to the limelight. She became the first Youth Poet Laureate of Los Angeles in 2014, and in 2017, she became the first-ever National Youth Poet Laureate in the U.S.

Before she stood at the Presidential podium on the West Front of the U.S. Capitol and read a poem for which she received national acclaim, Amanda had been in the public eye and rubbed shoulders with several public figures. In 2017, she introduced Hillary Clinton at a leadership awards gala. And while Michelle Obama was still First Lady, she recognized Amanda as a spoken word ambassador. Amanda was also interviewed by Oprah Winfrey on Zoom in 2020.

The Los Angeles Board of Library Commissioners honored Amanda with a special resolution and she was presented with an Outstanding Community Service Award by the City of Los Angeles. Her leadership was also recognized by the California State Assembly and mayor's office. She wrote the manifesto for Nike's 2020 Black History Month campaign, and her work has been featured in *The New York Times*, *The Wall Street Journal*, Elle.com, and *The Huffington Post*. She also received recognition from Scholastic, Inc. and the National YoungArts Foundation.

Amanda S.C. Gorman was born in Los Angeles, California on March 7, 1998. She has two siblings, including a twin sister named Gabrielle. All three were raised by a single mother, Joan Wicks, who taught 6th-grade English. Amanda began to write at a young age, and despite the speech impediment she developed in childhood and the auditory processing disorder she suffers—as well as her hypersensitivity to sound—she refined her literary voice over time and managed to express it with aplomb. Amanda studied sociology at Harvard, where she faced adversity from white classmates, one of whom—as she revealed in *The Harvard Crimson*—accused her of being "too strong and too self-assured." Aside from those experiences, Amanda considers her time at Harvard "an amazing privilege." While a high school senior, she was awarded the Milken Family Foundation college scholarship.

After reading her poem before an international audience, Amanda became an overnight success. Her Instagram following swelled, and she enjoyed enormous presales of her three books released in 2021. She became the first poet in history to be invited to read during a Super Bowl, which draws an audience of close to a billion fans. She also signed a modeling contract with IMG Models for brand endorsements and opportunities related to fashion. This is feasible given the fact that, as *The Guardian* reports:

"The red satin Prada headband she wore during the inauguration ceremony led to the item selling out, while her yellow coat (also Prada) caused searches for 'yellow coats' to increase 1,328% (according to fashion search engine Lyst) in the wake of her appearance." U

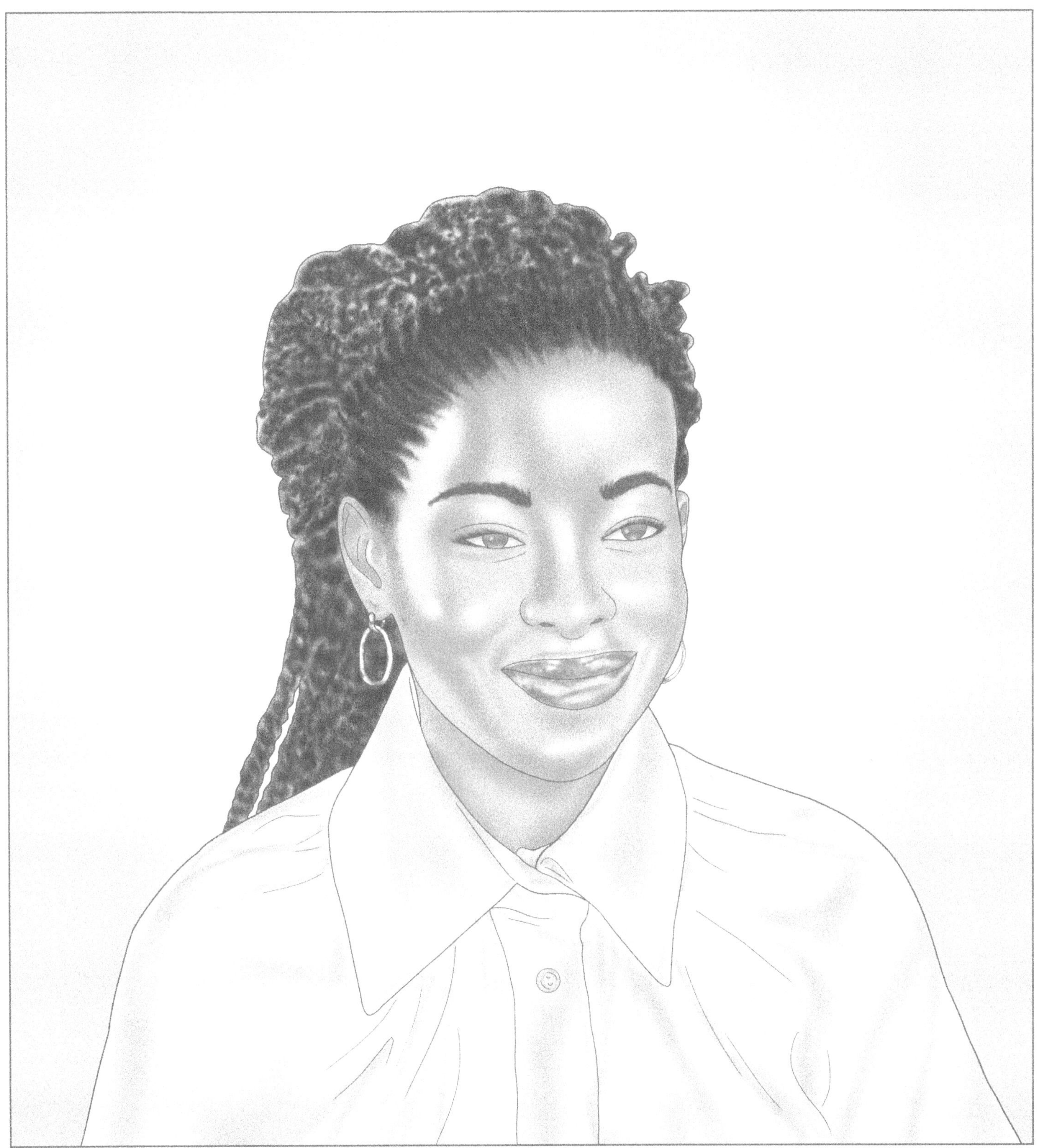

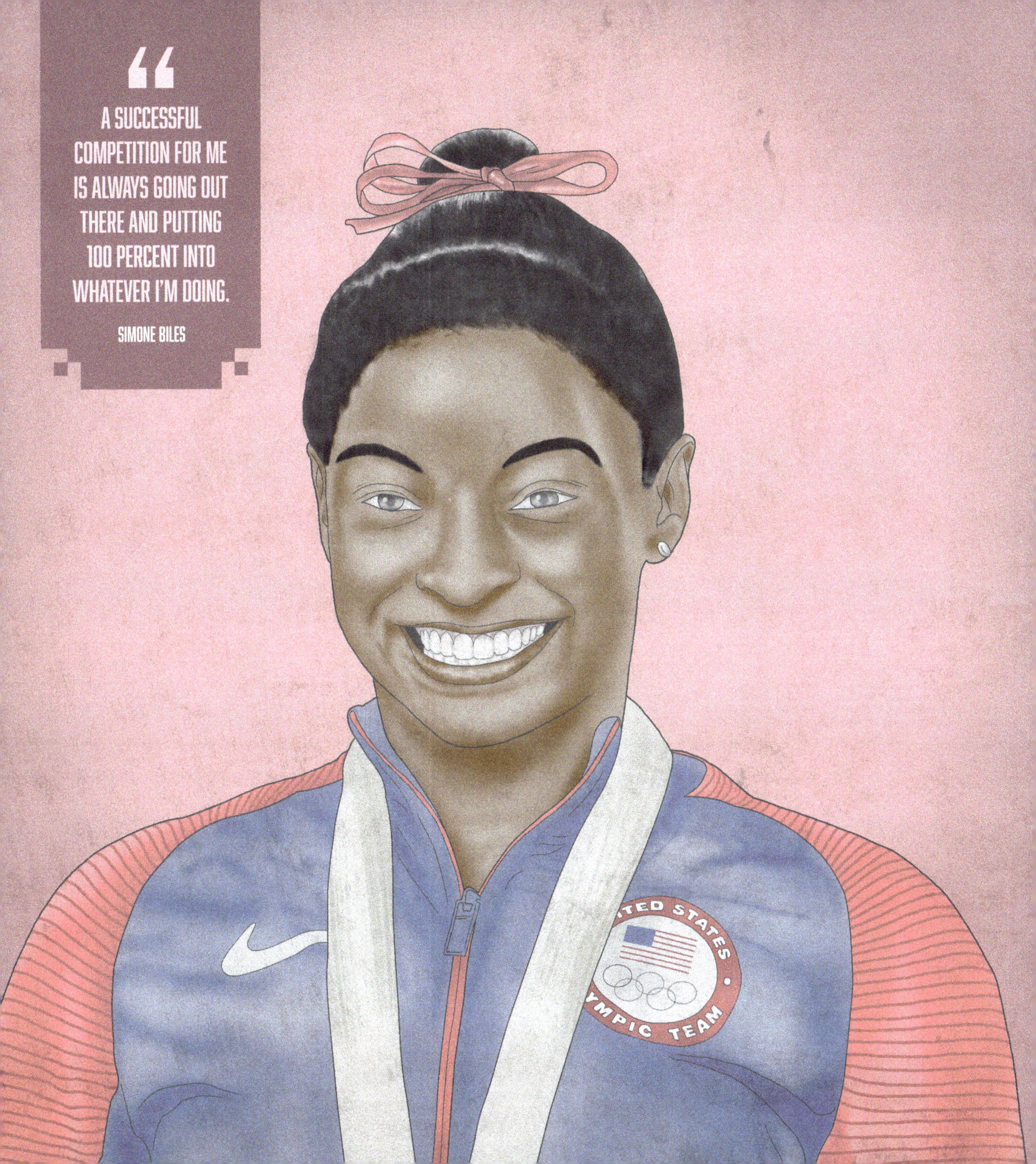
"
A SUCCESSFUL
COMPETITION FOR ME
IS ALWAYS GOING OUT
THERE AND PUTTING
100 PERCENT INTO
WHATEVER I'M DOING.

SIMONE BILES

SIMONE BILES

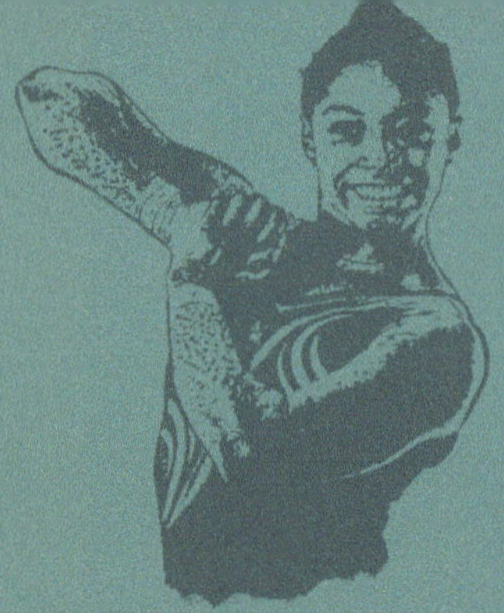

Simone Biles, the most decorated gymnast in U.S. history, has been shattering records since her entrance into the world of professional gymnastics. Her debut came in 2013, and with it, Biles has won every all-around competition she entered, be it team or individual. She is also the first woman to win three consecutive all-around titles in the history of World Gymnastics. Biles has won the most world medals in U.S. history and is the owner of more World Championship gold medals than any other gymnast. She is so dominant, U Sports reported:

"The other U.S. gymnasts joke that Biles is in her own class, therefore second place is still the winner."

Simone Arianne Biles was born in Columbus, Ohio on March 14, 1997. Biles is the third child of four. She has an older sister and brother—Ashley and Tevin—and a younger sister named Adria. Biles grew up in Spring, Texas, which is part of the Houston metropolitan area. She and her younger sister Adria were adopted from foster care by their grandparents, Ronald and Nellie Biles, who Biles considers to be her father and mother. When Biles was six, she went on a field trip to Bannon's Gymnastix in Houston, Texas, and showed a keen interest in the sport.

Biles had dabbled with gymnastics moves and had conquered the family trampoline, so by the time she arrived at Bannon's she was starry-eyed after seeing all the equipment that was just her size, everything from low beams and low bars to floor vaults. Biles started imitating a gymnast she saw do a back handspring, then she went from one apparatus to another copying other gymnasts. She was being watched the whole time, and a coach at the gym eventually came over to Biles and introduced herself. In her autobiography, *Courage to Soar: A Body in Motion, A Life in Balance*, Biles writes:

"That's how I arrived home from our field trip with a letter inviting me to enroll in gymnastics or tumbling classes at Bannon's."

Biles remained with Bannon's Gymnastix for 11 years and was coached by Aimee Boorman. In 2010, Biles won gold and bronze medals for the floor exercise and vault at the Women's Junior Olympic National Championships. She entered the elite level of competition the next year. By 2013, she would dominate professional gymnastics.

Biles is distinguished for her lively energy as well as the complexity she incorporates into her routines, be it uneven bars, vault, balance beam, or floor exercise. She not only thrives when it comes to individual routines, but she also led the U.S. Olympic women's gymnastics team, otherwise known as "The Final Five," to victory during the 2016 Summer Games. Biles made history by winning her 25th World Championship medal. She also has the most World Championship gold medals of any athlete, either male or female. Simone Biles usually wins by comparatively large margins when it comes to gymnastics scoring, but she continues to add layers of difficulty to the sport in the form of new skills and routines that raises the technical limits of professional gymnastics. U

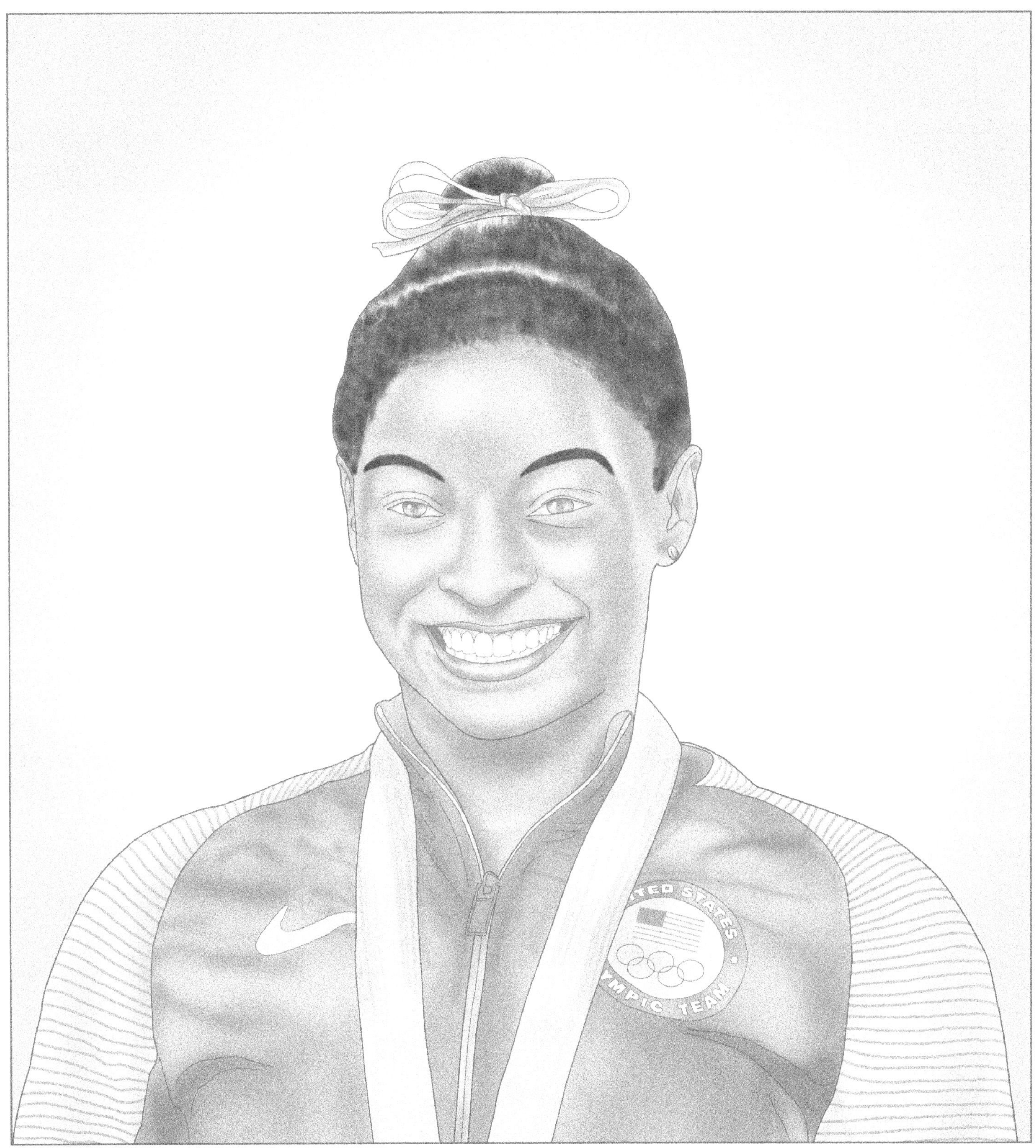

UNITED STATES
OLYMPIC TEAM

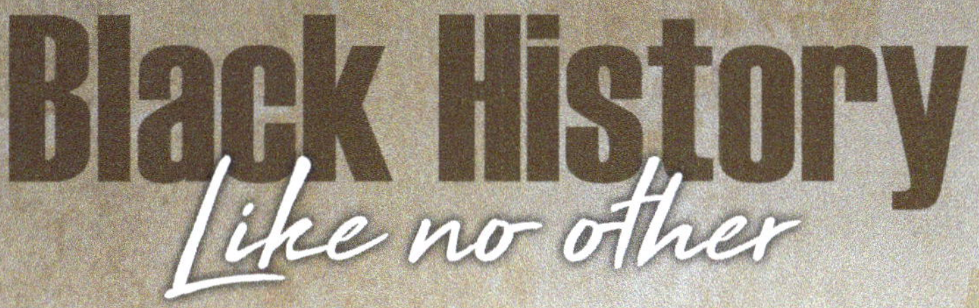

Black History
Like no other

Show your support by purchasing our title *The Black History Activity Book*. Packed with engaging articles, detailed coloring pages, puzzles, and more, you'll spend hours learning about hidden black history.

AVAILABLE FROM THESE RETAILERS: 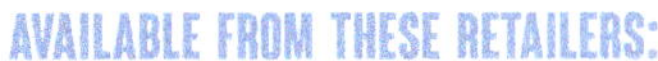

Learn more by scanning the QR code using the camera on your smartphone or tablet:

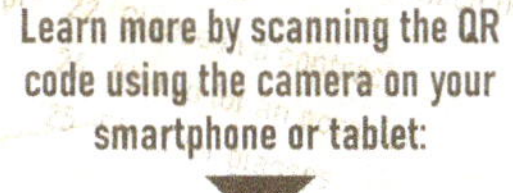